The Cure For
ONLYNESS

A Black Man's Guide To Joy, Passion & Purpose

COACH MICHAEL TAYLOR

Published by Creation Publishing Group LLC
www.creationpublishing.com

© 2019 Michael Taylor
ISBN # 978-0-9969487-9-1
Library of Congress Number # 2019910377

All rights reserved. No part of this book may be used or reproduced, stored in, or introduced into, a retrieval system, or transmitted in any form or by any means without the express written consent of the publisher.

Published and printed in the United States of America.

CONTENTS

Foreword
By Jewel Love 1

Acknowledgements 3

Introduction 5

Lesson One:
The Illness 11

Lesson Two:
The Cure 33

Lesson Three:
Embrace Science 53

Lesson Four:
Masculinity 73

Lesson Five:
Love 97

Lesson Six:
Health 117

Lesson Seven:
Wealth 127

Lesson Eight:
Spirituality 139

Lesson Nine:
Joy, Passion & Purpose 153

Lesson Ten:
Find Your Tribe 169

Takeaways 181

Resources 185

Bio 187

FOREWORD
By Jewel Love

Whether in the boardroom or among close friends, black men in Corporate America are walking a fine line. How do you open up and show your true self if you fear judgment from all sides? Better yet, how do you find out who you truly are inside?

The majority of my clients are radically successful in their professional life, having attended schools like Wharton, Harvard, and Stanford. Now leading teams at Apple, Google, and Microsoft. While their executive brain is turned on full throttle, they still feel a sense of Onlyness, and deep isolation.

While many reports to be "broken", like most of us, they never received an education that included emotional intelligence and psychological healing. By learning to look inside they realize the impacts of childhood wounds, reassess their abilities for grief and loss sensory, and learn how to better advocate for their own mental and emotional needs.

Showing up stronger in the workplace in life, they leave Onlyness behind, leading from a place of authenticity that binds them with all they choose to connect with.

There is a cure for Onlyness and Coach Michael Taylor is one of those guides for many black men seeking to leave the island of isolation and enter a new world of meaningful connections.

ACKNOWLEDGEMENTS

THERE ARE NO words that can come close to expressing the deep levels of joy and gratitude I feel as a result of my connection to a power greater than myself. I choose to call this power Divine Intelligence and it is my belief that this power created is also still creating this amazing Universe we live in. To this Divine Intelligence, I want to say a heartfelt thank you for loving me and for guiding me to find you and my divine purpose. I commit to using my gifts and talents in service to you and I dedicate my life to doing all I can to make the world a better place.

There was a time in my life when I was an Atheist and just the mention of the word God would turn me off and cause me to become defensive. At the time, there was nothing that could have been said which would have changed my mind. I was extremely rigid in my belief that God didn't exist and nothing could sway me from believing anything different.

It's been said skeptics make the best believers and after my 25-year journey to find my "truth" about God I must concur with that statement. Today, my belief in Divine Intelligence is the foundation of my life. I have evolved from just believing in Divine Intelligence to knowing that this power exists.

As I reflect over the past 25 years of my life I see nothing but miracles. I can see how every adversity and challenge in my life was perfectly orchestrated by Divine Intelligence to bring me to this exact moment in time. As a matter of fact, overcoming seemingly insurmountable obstacles is the reason my faith is so strong. I recognize there is no way I could have overcome all of the challenges in my life without some assistance from a power greater than myself and by surrendering to this truth. It allows me to know with absolute certainty that Divine Intelligence is always present.

I now know that Divine Intelligence has been preparing me to do extraordinary things in the world and I am now ready to fulfill my divine purpose and make a positive impact on the world. I feel blessed to know that I have been given some unique gifts and talents to help make the world a better place and I am committed to using those talents to positively impact the lives of people around the globe.

This book is one of the many ways I am using my gifts to impact the world and knowing this fills my heart with joy and gratitude.

So to all the men of color who are reading these words, know that you too have access to this Divine Intelligence. It is your responsibility to develop a deep intimacy and connection to this power and once you do nothing will be impossible for you.

So I would like to acknowledge each of you and let you know just how proud I am of you for taking the time to read this book and my prayer is the wisdom I share will support you in creating an extraordinary life for yourself. Upon completion, if you will apply the lessons learned you would then have the tools of awareness to create the life you were born to live.

You got this, so let's do it!

INTRODUCTION

While scrolling through my LinkedIn news feed I ran across a comment by Jewel Love that caught my attention and stopped me in my tracks. Jewel is a therapist in California that specializes in working with high net worth professional black men in corporate America and he runs an organization called Executive Black Men.

The comment said: "Onlyness" is the #1 mental health concern for many Black Executive Men."

I had not heard the term Onlyness before but it resonated with me so deeply that I spent several minutes reflecting on its meaning. As I sat there thinking about it I realized that it spoke directly to how I've felt most of my life. It is a feeling that arises from being the only person of color in business environments and social settings. It comes up when you're the only one from your close group of childhood friends that climbs the corporate ladder and becomes financially successful. You experience it when you put together a stable family environment with little to no drama and you watch other members of your family struggle with the challenges of raising a family. It's about the feeling of disconnection we sometimes feel if we choose to do something that isn't "Black enough". It's about breaking free from labels and embracing our humanness, which leads to becoming fully authentic, in who we are.

It's a unique feeling because it is a combination of loneliness, sadness, anger and happiness.

The loneliness comes from the feelings of isolation of being the only person of color in the room at times. The sadness comes from knowing you will automatically be judged based on the color of your skin and not the content of your character. The anger comes from knowing you will have to work twice as hard to accomplish certain things and you know the color of your skin is the reason why. And yet the happiness is there because you know deep down inside you can handle it all. Something inside of you lets you know that you are the captain of your own ship and the master of your own destiny.

There is a part of you that knows despite every obstacle that has been placed in front of black men we have found a way to overcome them and thrive. There is an inner joy and happiness that comes from knowing this. You know at a soul level that the strength of your ancestors is encoded in your DNA and you draw upon that strength to get you through the tough times.

It is this inner knowing that has allowed me to overcome the Onlyness in my own life and allowed me to create my version of an extraordinary one that far exceeds what society says a man of color with only an 11th-grade education should have accomplished.

What I have learned over the past 25 years as a writer and speaker is there is a cure for Onlyness. Without question, every black man is capable of creating an extraordinary life if he chooses. But to do so, we must create a new conversation amongst ourselves about what is possible. We must embrace a sense of optimism and infinite possibilities for our lives. We must begin by educating ourselves about ourselves and understand that no one or nothing can keep us from accomplishing our dreams except us.

Despite the obvious challenges facing black men today, I am extremely optimistic about our future. It is my belief and contention that there has never been a better time to be alive on this planet than right now and the future is filled with infinite possibilities for those of us who are willing to put forth the effort.

This book is written as an empowerment guide to support you in creating joy, passion and purpose in your life. If you will follow the suggestions within its pages I am absolutely certain you can overcome Onlyness and build the life of your dreams.

Introduction

To do so, apply the wisdom contained in these pages and remember the immortal words of the great Maya Angelo; "Still I Rise!"

Good luck! I'll see you on the flip side of Onlyness, which is Connection!

STILL I RISE
BY MAYA ANGELOU

You may write me down in history
With your bitter, twisted lies,
You may trod me in the very dirt
But still, like dust, I'll rise.

Does my sassiness upset you?
Why are you beset with gloom?
'Cause I walk like I've got oil wells
Pumping in my living room.

Just like moons and like suns,
With the certainty of tides,
Just like hopes springing high,
Still, I'll rise.

Did you want to see me broken?
Bowed head and lowered eyes?
Shoulders falling down like teardrops,
Weakened by my soulful cries?

Does my haughtiness offend you?
Don't you take it awful hard
'Cause I laugh like I've got gold mines
Diggin' in my own backyard.

You may shoot me with your words,
You may cut me with your eyes,
You may kill me with your hatefulness,
But still, like air, I'll rise.

Does my sexiness upset you?
Does it come as a surprise
That I dance like I've got diamonds
At the meeting of my thighs?

Out of the huts of history's shame
I rise
Up from a past, that's rooted in pain
I rise
I'm a black ocean, leaping and wide,
Welling and swelling I bear in the tide.

Leaving behind nights of terror and fear
I rise
Into a daybreak that's wondrously clear
I rise
Bringing the gifts that my ancestors gave,
I am the dream and the hope of the slave.
I rise
I rise
I rise.

Everything that is faced cannot be changed, but nothing can be changed until it is faced.

James Baldwin

LESSON ONE:
The Illness

Back in 1994, I was having lunch at a restaurant when I happened to overhear a conversation between two well-dressed, well-spoken and apparently well educated young black men. They were having a conversation about the eradication of black men from America and I must admit the conversation broke my heart. They were discussing how difficult it was for black men to make it in America and they had made up their minds that America was a racist country that was doing everything in its power to keep black men from succeeding.

After listening for a few moments I decided to approach their table and confront them about the conversation they were having. I apologized for eavesdropping and I then asked the men if they truly believed what they were saying. One of the men looked at me with a look that I will never forget. He had the most powerless, defeated, frustrated and depressed look I'd ever seen. His body language and tone of voice screamed out "I am a victim of society".

I then asked him if he truly believed everything they were talking about and he said something that stopped me in my tracks. He looked me dead in the eyes and said: "absolutely I believe what I said. Don't you watch the news? I believe in 20 years all black men are going to be dead or in jail!"

I will never forget the look on his face, the sound of his voice or the conviction in which he expressed his beliefs and feelings about the status of black men in America. It almost brought me to tears. As I looked at him with deep compassion and sympathy I knew there was nothing I could have said to change his mind so I placed my hand on his shoulder and simply said: "don't believe the hype my brother, don't believe the hype" and I walked away. As I was walking away, there was something inside of me that knew I needed to do something. I had no idea what, but deep down inside of me I knew I had to do something to help change the mindset of black men in America.

As a result of that conversation, I decided to become a writer and speaker so I could share the lessons I've learned during my own inner journey of transformation with other men of color to support them on their journey.

My journey has allowed me to overcome being a high school dropout who also experienced divorce, bankruptcy, foreclosure a deep state of depression and even being homeless for 2 years living out of a car. Overcoming these obstacles and now being an entrepreneur, author, motivational speaker, radio & TV host gives me the credibility and authority to say that anything is possible if you set your mind to it and my mission is to inspire black men to recognize this truth.

I've written four books targeted specifically to men of color to support them in overcoming the multiplicity of challenges we face and my goal has been to simply change the mindset of black men around the globe.

After more than 25 years as a writer who has written a total of 8 books dealing with personal growth and development, I have concluded that "The Illness" that inflicts far too many black men is the illness of a negative mindset and attitude. It is this illness that keeps black men from succeeding and reaching their full potential. It is this illness that keeps black men from creating great relationships and having financial abundance. It is this illness that keeps black men from experiencing joy, passion and purpose. Until you fully understand, what you think about, you bring about, you will never be able to overcome this illness so this is the primary reason you should be reading this book. So you can learn how to guard the gates of your mind and make sure that you learn to be optimistic and maintain a positive mental attitude.

So you may be wondering, how and why do so many black men contract this illness of a negative mindset and attitude?

I'll use a metaphor to explain.

Lesson One: The Illness

I'd like you to imagine a river of flowing water. There are mountains all around and there are beautiful flowers, plants and trees everywhere. It looks like paradise. Now imagine there are people floating along on inner tubes down this river. Everyone is simply going with the flow and moving in the direction of the river's current. Let's call this river the Drift.

The drift is a metaphor for society. Most people are floating along with this societal current of conformity and they are completely oblivious to the fact they are trapped in this flow.

Now I would like you to imagine that everyone on the inner tubes is white. Therefore the collective consciousness of the drift is based on a "white" way of thinking. I call it the CWBS. The Collective White Belief System. The CWBS is a rigid way of thinking in which the collective consciousness believes its way of thinking is the "right" way of thinking. Any other way of thinking is seen as a threat and therefore rejected by the CWBS.

Herein lies the problem. We live in a society and culture based primarily on the CWBS.

Ever since black people were brought to this country the CWBS has dictated how black people were treated and what they could or could not do. It was the CWBS that instituted laws that kept black people from learning how to read and then proposed that black people were less intelligent than white people. It was the CWBS that caused some white people to believe they were superior to blacks so they created organizations that attempted to eradicate black people from this county in an attempt to maintain the CWBS.

It was the CWBS that proposed segregation laws to keep races separate and instituted anti-miscegenation laws to keep people of different races from marrying each other.

The CWBS is a collective way of thinking based on the majority of people in the US, which by the way happens to be white. Since the majority of people who own mainstream media happen to be white there has always been a slanted bias in their reporting of stories towards people of color because the CWBS has always promoted that we as black people are somehow different than white people.

Therefore, the media has always implied that black people are the major causes of the social ills impacting our country. For example, when you think about poverty, chances are you think of a black family in the inner city projects on food stamps or government assistance. However, the majority of people on food stamps and on government assistance happen to be white.

To put it simply, the CWBS creates the beliefs most people hold on to and when you believe something strongly enough those beliefs become your reality. Therefore, when you pay attention to mainstream media it creates "beliefs" that are either accepted or rejected to those who tune in to mainstream media.

Side note:

This is the reason I believe America is no longer a racist country. I understand this country still has residual residue from its racist past and there are still racists policies that create an unfair "system", but a society is simply a reflection of the consciousness of its people and it is my belief that the majority of people are not racists. In other words, the people floating along in the drift are changing their minds and the majority of them are no longer racists. There are some people who believe in a tipping point in consciousness in which the collective consciousness will shift. Some believe once a belief is changed in 51% of the people it creates a new belief system in the entire collective . I believe that tipping point was reached during the civil rights movement and that shift in consciousness continues to this day. Collectively speaking, America isn't racist but without question there are still remnants of racist policies and the system is still unjust and unfair and it is definitely still biased.

In the case of the two black men, the CWBS media created a belief in the young men's mind that black men were an endangered species and they obviously accepted those beliefs and were acting consistently with those beliefs based on their conversation.

It's important to understand there are three primary sources that shape our beliefs and attitudes about ourselves and the world around us.

1. Our families
2. Our cultures
3. Our societies.

If you come from a loving nurturing family, chances are you will have loving nurturing beliefs. If you are raised in a violent and dangerous culture, it is possible you will have violent and angry beliefs. If you live in a society that constantly bombards you with negative images of yourself and your culture, chances are you will have negative beliefs about yourself and your culture.

This is what happened for the two young men in the restaurant. Remember what he said: "don't you watch the news?" The media created a belief in his mind that all black men were going to be dead or in jail in 20 years. Obviously, that belief didn't materialize and I wonder what he would say if I spoke with him today, but at the time, the guy was absolutely convinced black men were being eradicated and there was nothing I could have said that would have changed his mind at that time. This is the power of the illness of a negative mindset and attitude.

You see, society (the media) convinced them to believe black men have too many obstacles in front of them and therefore they may as well give up and feel victimized. Since thoughts become things, what do you think having that negative mindset about black men would have created in that mans life? I will suggest their negative mindset would have definitely caused a lot of fear and anxiety in their lives and a deep feeling of powerlessness and victimization. If a person truly feels that way how likely are they to accomplish remarkable things in their lives? Not likely! That's why it's so important to recognize this illness so you can change your mindset and attitude to be more positive and optimistic.

What's important to understand is your beliefs create your mindset and attitude. So take a moment and think about some of the messages we receive as black men.

When we watch unarmed black men being killed by police what beliefs do you think we create about ourselves? We are expendable? Our lives are worthless? We are powerless? Society is trying to eradicate us?

When we see stories like The Central Park Five in which five young black men were falsely accused of rape and were vilified by the media for a crime they didn't commit, what does that do to our psyches? Do we create a belief that the system is definitely stacked against us and there is nothing we can do about it? Do we create a belief that all white people hate us and want to see us incarcerated?

When we are constantly portrayed as thugs and gangsters that desert our children and disrespect our women what negative impact does that have on our beliefs about ourselves?

And what about the CBBS? The Collective Black Belief System. How does it affect our belief systems when we are constantly told that black people are caught up in "The Struggle" and we live in a racist society that is doing everything in its power to keep us from living our dreams?

The CBBS can be just as devastating to our mindset as the CWBS. When we are accused of being sellouts for doing things that may not be considered "black enough" we are trapped in the CBBS. The CBBS creates a "black box" in which all black people are supposed to fit into and if you do not fit in and assimilate, your black card may get revoked.

The lesson here is your mindset and attitude are the keys to your success. It's important to understand the origin of our beliefs but it's more important to understand that you actually have complete control over how and what you think. In other words, if you are trapped in the illness of a negative mindset and attitude you have the ability to change. There is a powerful quote from the good book that says; "As a man thinketh in his heart so shall he be." This is the lesson I want you to remember from this chapter.

There is a guy named Mike Dooley who wrote a book titled Thoughts Become Things. It is a wonderful book that talks about

Lesson One: The Illness

the importance of how our thoughts actually shape and create our reality. The primary message is exactly what the title suggests. So take a moment and ask yourself what are you thinking about yourself as a man of color? What beliefs are you holding on to that may be keeping you from creating the life you know you deserve?

Here is a quick exercise that if you will be honest with yourself and complete it, it will give you an opportunity to truly examine some of your deeply held unconscious beliefs about black men.

Get a timer (or use your phone) and a sheet of paper. At the top of the page write

Black men are…

Set your timer for 60 seconds. Then without thinking about it simply write down as quickly as possible everything that comes to mind. Keep writing for 60 seconds without stopping. Be completely honest with yourself. Do not filter your answers. Just write down whatever thoughts you have. You do not have to share this with anyone. It's just for you to see. If you will be completely honest with yourself it will let you see how the CWBS and the CBBS has influenced your beliefs about black men.

Do not worry if your answers are positive or negative. Just be honest. Tell yourself your truth about how you see black men. Once you get your beliefs on paper then you can make a decision to change them if you'd like. But the key is to bring them from your subconscious mind to your conscious mind so you can change them. You cannot change a belief if you are unaware that you have them so it's important to do this exercise to bring the belief into your awareness.

After more than 25 years of research, I am absolutely confident that anyone can change their mindset and attitudes if they choose to. It can be challenging but without question it is doable. Like any illness, a negative mindset and attitude can be cured and we will be discussing specific ways to do that in the next chapter. In the meantime, this simple exercise can actually be a part of the cure for a negative mindset and attitude.

Now let's go back to the CWBS metaphor. Imagine all of the white people floating down the Drift. They each have a belief about black men and collectively those beliefs are negative. Those negative beliefs become stereotypes, which are then shared amongst the people in the drift and ultimately throughout the media. Now mainstream media embraces these stereotypes and they begin spreading them through mainstream news. If you happen to be white, chances are you may have no personal interaction with black men so your beliefs about them will come from the media and since the media generally shows the negative stereotypes about black men. What do you think your beliefs are going to be about then? Negative of course!

Unfortunately, the same beliefs are sometimes accepted by men of color and that is the reason we must become aware of them.

I would now like to share 10 CWBS stereotypes about black men that have been perpetuated for a very long time. These stereotypes will keep you from accomplishing your goals and creating an extraordinary life. These are the 10 most destructive media generated illusions about black men that I wrote about in my previous book titled Shattering Black Male Stereotypes.

(I highly recommend that you add it to your list of must-read books. See www.shatteringblackmalestereotypes.com)

If you are truly committed to living a life of joy, passion and purpose you must make sure you are aware of these stereotypes and you do not accept them.

Illusion #1 ~ Black Men Are An Endangered Species

Illusion #2 ~ Black Men Use Race As an Excuse for Failure

Illusion #3 ~ Black Men Try To Be White

Illusion #4 ~ Black Men Are Less Intelligent

Illusion #5 ~ Black Men Are Angry and Violent

Illusion #6 ~ Black Men Cannot Be Monogamous

Illusion #7 ~ Black Men Are Deadbeat Dads

Illusion #8 ~ Black Men Are Physically/Sexually Superior

Illusion #9 ~ Black Men Are Not Patriotic

Illusion #10 ~ Black Men Are Lazy

So let's break them down and bring them up from your subconscious mind into your conscious mind so you can remove them if needed.

Illusion #1 ~ Black Men Are an Endangered Species

This is the reason the men in the restaurant were having a negative conversation. Too many men of color actually believe this and it is one of the most destructive beliefs a black man can hold on to. I facilitated an online empowerment summit based on these stereotypes and one of the participants sent me an email thanking me for making him aware of this stereotype. He said the majority of his life he had accepted this belief and felt completely victimized by society. He said he didn't believe he would live to be 50 years old because he was afraid that either he was going to be killed by someone in his neighborhood or by a police officer. After he listened to the summit he had a change of heart and decided he was responsible for changing his life and he said he felt a sense of optimism he had never experienced. He explained how grateful he was for hearing a black man talk about being optimistic and having a positive mental attitude and he said he was committed to changing his mindset so he could change his life.

So let me set the record straight. There is no threat to the survival of black men in this country. Contrary to mainstream media we are actually positioned to experience unprecedented levels of success in society today. This is evidenced by the fact that there is no segment of society that does not have a black male presence. We are CEO's, authors, speakers, dentists, chiropractors, attorneys, graphic-artists, astronauts, doctors, chemists, astrophysicists and we've even been president of the United States. There is no position in society that does not have a black male presence. So rest assured we are not an endangered species and the future is filled with infinite possibilities for those of us who are willing to put forth the effort and make it happen.

Illusion #2 ~ Black Men Use Race As an Excuse for Failure

I have definitely had conversations with black men who believe their race is the cause of their failure, but for the most part, I believe most black men do not blame their race for their failures. Yes, we have been passed over for jobs and denied opportunities as a result of our skin color. Yes, we have to deal with the fact that we are judged by the color of our skin not the content of our character. Yes, we may have to work twice as hard to earn the same respect (and money) as white people. Although this may be unfair we keep pressing forward and blazing new trails despite the obstacles we have to overcome.

As a man who has dealt with racial discrimination all of his life, I can understand why some black men feel powerless in this country. Without question racism and discrimination are both alive and well, and yet, black men continue to make strides in a country that appears to be doing everything it can to keep them from succeeding.

If you are committed to living an extraordinary life (which I'm sure is the case if you're reading this book) it's imperative for you to understand that you are 100% responsible for your life turning out the way you want it to and you cannot use race as an excuse if you aren't living the life you were born to live.

So remember the words of George Washington Carver, "Ninety-nine percent of the failures come from people who have the habit of making excuses."

So it's okay to call out racism and discrimination for what it is. But at the same time know that you cannot use race as an excuse for your failures. If you want something badly enough no one or nothing can keep you from getting it except yourself.

Illusion #3 ~ Black Men Try To Be White

This stereotype is actually driven by the CBBS. For most of my life, I have been called a sellout simply because I've chosen to do things that were considered "not black". When I was in high school I loved to surf and ride skateboards. I also enjoyed rock music and would sometimes blast it on my car stereo. I was attacked and criticized for trying to be white because of these choices. As an adult, I love participating in personal development seminars and in a lot of cases I am the only man of color in the seminar. Amazing writers who aren't black fill my library with books and I listen to a host of speakers and coaches who inspires me and challenges me to become the best version of my Self.

I have had heated discussions with black friends who ask why I seldom read books by black authors. For example, I never read books about slavery or black history. I've never read the Autobiography of Malcolm X and I have no interest in reading The New Jim Crow or Between The World and Me. I do not want to negate the importance of these books, I simply choose not to read books that do not teach me something about myself to help me become a better person. I do not need to read a book about something that I have first-hand experience and knowledge of. I do not have to read a book about racism or slavery to understand their impact on black people. I deal with the ramifications of these things on a daily basis. The only criteria I use when choosing to read a book or attend a seminar is will this book/seminar help me become the best version of myself? If the answer is yes I'm open to reading it. I don't care who wrote it or who is facilitating it. If I can learn something that improves the quality of my life, count me in.

Therefore, it's important to dispel this stereotype head-on. Your first responsibility is to yourself. You are not bound by your race to have to do anything. You have this amazing gift called choice and you get to choose what's right for yourself. Rest assured you are only a sellout if you allow others to dictate what you can or cannot do. You are the captain of your own ship and the master of your own destiny. Do not be afraid to be called a sellout if you are doing things that nurture your spirit and helps you become a better human being.

The real question isn't who is not going to let you live the life of your dreams; the question is, who is going to stop you? Don't let anyone stop you. Not even yourself.

Illusion #4 ~ Black Men Are Less Intelligent

Ever since black people were brought to this country the CWBS has done everything it could to prove that black people were somehow less intelligent than whites. There were (and still are) so-called 'experts' that attempt to prove that we were genetically inferior based on science. There were organizations that proposed that black people had smaller brains than white people and were therefore incapable of being as smart as whites. Even today, there are still a lot of people who argue the case that we are intellectually inferior.

Although times have changed for the better and we have made great strides in race relations in this country, there is still the implied stereotype that black men are *less intelligent* than other men.

So lets set the record straight. There is no scientific evidence to support this ludicrous idea. As human beings, we all have an infinite capacity for learning and growing and we're responsible for committing to constant and never ending improvement in our lives. The real question you must ask yourself is, are you willing to grow intellectually? Or you committed to learning new things and reaching your full potential? It's been said knowledge is power, which is true, but incomplete. Applied knowledge is power, so commit to learning as much as you can and then apply your knowledge to and take action on your dreams and then you will have authentic power.

Illusion #5 ~ Black Men Are Angry and Violent

Here is an excerpt from my book Shattering Black Male Stereotypes that speaks directly to this particular stereotype.

"Unfortunately, some news outlets make generalizations about groups of people based on the color of their skin, specifically the black community, in order to boost ratings." - SaiNagula

This is exactly what the CWBS does. In order to boost ratings, it focuses on sensationalizing stories by making generalizations about groups of people based on their skin color. In other words, the CWBS perpetuates the illusion that black men are violent and angry because the media knows that's what its customers want to see.

Lesson One: The Illness

The sad part is that far too many of our black males buy into this stereotype, and they put on these masks of being hard, rigid and tough when in reality they can be sad, scared, or confused.

Generally speaking, regardless of race, men have been conditioned to believe that it's not OK to feel. From a very young age, we are taught that big boys/real men don't cry or show emotion because that is a sign of weakness.

Herein lies the real problem. When we teach our young men to disconnect from their emotions and feelings, it removes their ability to create intimacy and connection with others, which leads to unhealthy relationships. In order to be relational, a man must first be emotional and this is the only way for a man to create authentic fulfilling relationships.

Too many black men are not emotionally equipped to create an authentic connection in relationships, and a lot of this is the result of accepting the media-generated stereotypes that suggest black men are always angry.

So, let's set the record straight: black men do not have a monopoly on anger or violence. We have the same feelings and emotions as any other group of men. We are definitely capable of creating emotionally connected and intimate relationships that truly nurture us. We feel love and compassion, sadness and disappointment, joy and sorrow, we feel empathy and experience true intimacy. Once again, I state we are no different than any other group of men despite what the CWBS may show you through the media.

Illusion #6 ~ Black Men Cannot Be Monogamous

If you pay attention to music videos and mainstream media it should be easy to see how this stereotype is perpetuated. We are constantly bombarded with half naked women at strip clubs being admired and adored for their physical bodies with no thought to their true essence and lovability on the inside. We see men "making it rain" by throwing money at them and seeking to have sex with them with no thought of emotional intimacy or emotional connection. One rapper declared, " I am into having sex I'm not into making love" which promotes the idea that our job as men is to simply have sex with women with no emotional connection. Collectively speaking men who have multiple sex partners are looked upon as heroes and a man who chooses to love only one woman and choose monogamy is seen as being "pussy whipped" and attached to a ball and chain. Somehow being monogamous is seen as something only weak men do and being a "playa" and sleeping with as many women as possible is what most men prefer.

It is my belief that most men actually do want to be monogamous. I believe men truly crave intimacy and connection yet very few of them know how to do this. If a man is completely honest with himself I believe he will admit that he wants to find that special person to share his life with and has no interest in trying to juggle multiple relationships at the same time. Not only is it emotionally draining but it also has a financial impact that empties a man's wallet which I know men dislike.

In summary, every man is capable of being monogamous. Monogamy is a choice and without question, there are lots of us who choose the path of monogamy and we are definitely happy and content with that choice. So if you believe black men cannot be monogamous think again. We can and we are.

Illusion #7 ~ Black Men Are Deadbeat Dads

When a person hears the term deadbeat dad I would suggest the first thing that comes to mind would be a black male. The CWBS bombards us with stories and images of irresponsible black men, which causes the belief we do not love or take care of our children. Nothing could be farther from the truth. As black men, we love and nurture our children no less than any other group of men. We are capable of developing deep, loving, caring and nurturing relationships with our children and the majority of us actually play an important part in our children's lives.

Instead of attacking the CWBS for their portrayal of us as deadbeat dads we must commit to becoming great fathers and break the generational curses that may be keeping us from doing so. This means we must understand that being a great father isn't genetic. There is no such thing as a good father gene. Being a great father is learned behavior, which means any man can learn to become a great father even if he didn't have a great role model as a father.

Illusion #8 ~ Black Men Are Physically/Sexually Superior

If you pay attention to mainstream media you may have concluded black men are physically superior to other athletes. This is in part to how the media adores athletes and generally highlights the accomplishments of black men because of their raw physical talent. Since the two most popular sports in America are football and basketball and black men make up the majority of the teams, it's easy to see how this stereotype gets perpetuated.

The truth is we are not physically superior. Pro athletes are the exception, not the rule and though we may dominate major sports, collectively we are not superior. Anytime a particular race claims to be superior it borders on racism so there is no need for us to make that claim. The good news is we have an opportunity to showcase our physical athleticism through sports and in some ways that is a good stereotype to have. The downside is, even though we may dominate in sports we unfortunately, lead the nation in most health related illnesses and death, which is truly an ironic paradox.

In regards to sexual superiority, there is this stereotype that all black men are hung to their knees and are sexually superior and better loves than men of other races. This too is a stereotype and illusion and though it appears to be a compliment, if we look a little deeper it isn't. The over-sexualized black male is a stereotype that ties into the stereotype that black men can't be monogamous and therefore it is a stereotype which we should not be proud of.

Illusion #9 ~ Black Men Are Not Patriotic

This stereotype was definitely highlighted when Colin Kaepernick decided not to stand for the national anthem at the beginning of NFL games during the 2016 NFL season. His protest launched an attack from the president of the United States who misinterpreted and reframed the protest into disrespecting the flag and our military (even though that was never the purpose of the protest), which began a powerful backlash from a lot of conservatives. Of course this is a divisive issue but it definitely isn't new. Black men have been accused of not being patriotic anytime they take a stand (or a knee) against injustice. I'm reminded of the 1968 Olympics in which Tommy Smith and John Carlos raised their fists in protest of the lynching's that were taking place in America. They began as heroes by winning medals in the 200-yard dash, but they instantly became villains after their protest and were suspended from the national team, expelled from the Olympic village and sent home to the United States.

Which begs the question; what does it mean to be patriotic? When an American is protesting the killing of other Americans by Americans does that mean he is being unpatriotic? Herein lies the great hypocrisy of the CWBS. A patriot can be defined as "a person who loves, supports, and defends his or her country and its interests with devotion. a person who regards himself or herself as a defender, especially of individual rights, against presumed interference by the federal government." I believe this describes Colin Kaepernick, Tommy Smith and John Carlos to a T. They were protesting because they love this country and they were trying to ensure that every American was safe from murder from other Americans.

By protesting the killing of innocent Americans, by definition, weren't they being patriots? I believe the answer is yes. Of course, this is definitely a heated topic and everyone is entitled to his or her opinion. My belief is we love this country as black men and we are willing to do whatever it takes to make sure this country loves us back even when it appears it doesn't.

I was so moved by Colin Kaepernicks protest I put my thoughts together and wrote a piece for the Huffington Post to express my support of his right to protest. Here is the piece I wrote.

Is Colin Kaepernick Hurting or Helping Black Men in America?

As America continues to be divided by Colin Kaepernick's refusal to stand during the national anthem at his San Francisco 49ers football games, this story sheds light on the complexities of being a black man in America.

I'm reminded of a quote by Dr. Steven Covey from his bestselling book, The 7 Habits of Highly Effective People in which he stated, *"seek first to understand, and then be understood."* This quote truly captures how American society could address race relations going forward, and use Colin's protest as an opportunity for growth and transformation.

At first glance, it is understandable why so many people are upset about Colin not standing for the national anthem. To some, it appears that he is disrespecting the flag and his country. But if we are willing to look a little deeper and try to understand his motives, hopefully, it can change the perception of what he is attempting to do.

As I am reminded of the incidences of police brutality against black men in this country, I can immediately empathize with Colin's protest. I can relate to his anger, frustration, and sadness about watching too many men of color needlessly lose their lives, and then have their perpetrators walk away without being held accountable for their actions. Understanding breeds compassion, and if we are willing to simply see this point of view, then we can recognize that this is the core of his protest. No matter how the media attempts to frame Colin's demonstration, I believe this is the primary reason he refuses to stand. This leads us to the question: Is Colin's protest unpatriotic? Herein lies the great American hypocrisy. The dictionary defines a patriot as: *a person who vigorously supports their country and is prepared to defend it against enemies or detractors.* Isn't this exactly what Colin is attempting to do? He recognizes that American citizens are being killed and he is taking a stand against this crisis. How can this be viewed as unpatriotic? His actions are the highest form of patriotism. He is willing to not only sacrifice his livelihood for what he believes, but he is also actually willing to put his life on the line (he has received several death threats) in an attempt to make America better by bringing attention to the fact that too many men of color are being senselessly and unnecessarily killed.

According to Mike Freeman of Bleacher Report (www.bleacherreport.com), several NFL league officials actually hate Colin and his stance. Here are just a few quotes from top NFL officials: *"I don't want him anywhere near my team,"* one executive told Freeman. *"He's a traitor,"* said another exec. *"He has no respect for our country. F— that guy."* And from a general manager, *"In my career, I have never seen a guy so hated by front office guys as Kaepernick."*

So, is it patriotic for a man to be hated simply because he is attempting to stop the killing of innocent Americans? Think about that for a moment.

In regards to the military, this is what they fight for. Servicemen and women fight for our right to speak out, defend our country, and use our freedom of speech to help improve this country. They aren't fighting for us to be silent when it comes to addressing issues within the confines of America. If we aren't willing to speak out to make America better, should that not be considered unpatriotic?

In a lot of ways, the Colin Kaepernick story is a microcosm of being a black man in America. On one hand, if we take a stand and speak out against social injustice, we are accused of being angry black men who hate America. On the other hand, if we aren't attempting to resolve the problems in our own communities, we are called lazy and indifferent to the challenges of black men in America.

As I've watched and listened to some of the opinions voiced

Lesson One: The Illness

by black men, I can only imagine how difficult it must be for Colin. There are some black men who attacked and vilified him for his stance while others embraced and supported his decision to protest. As a man who happens to be black, I can definitely relate to this conundrum. For most of my life, I have been accused of being a sellout because of my optimism and belief that nothing is impossible if you put your mind to it, even if you're black. I have been criticized, ostracized, and accused of being blind to the challenges facing black men in this country. Sometimes it feels like a no-win situation. But you can't please everyone, so it's important to be clear on what you stand for and not be affected by the thoughts and opinions of others.

And now I would like to answer the question I posed at the beginning: Is Colin Kaepernick hurting or helping black men in America? I believe he is definitely helping black men, and more broadly, he is helping America. I say this because his actions have ignited a debate about police brutality and a few years from now, I believe he will be recognized and acknowledged for his willingness to take a stand (or in this case a knee) against an issue that has been pushed under the American rug for far too long. The time has come to face this challenge head-on so that we cannot only eradicate police brutality but also bridge some of the racial divides in this country.

To be clear, I disagree with several of Colin's points in regards to this issue. But first and foremost, I completely agree with his right to protest, and I commend him for his courage to do so. Thank you, Colin Kaepernick for teaching me that you do not necessarily have to stand up in order to love your country. You can kneel and love your country even when most people around you will accuse you of being a traitor.

In conclusion, I believe most black men actually love this country, I know I do, and despite the atrocities we've had to endure, I still believe in America and will do everything I can to support her in living up to her highest potential.

Illusion #10 ~ Black Men Are Lazy

I will not even dignify this stereotype with a response. Our successes dispute this stereotype automatically. Rest assured it isn't true. So just be sure you are doing whatever it takes for you to build the life of your dreams and know that you have everything you need inside of you already to do so. Don't be lazy! Get out there and make your dreams come true.

So those are the 10 most destructive media generated illusions about black men. If you believe any of them it means you are trapped in the "Illness" and it's time to change your mindset and your attitude. Make sure you do not believe any of them and most importantly, make sure you are not acting consistently with any of them. Be willing to challenge any negative deeply held beliefs you may be holding on to about black men and commit yourself to constantly removing any limiting or negative beliefs about yourself and about black men.

Your take away from this chapter should be the impact the CWBS has had on your belief systems and yet, you must realize you have complete control over your own mind and your beliefs. The CWBS cannot control how you think. When you take complete control of your beliefs, thoughts and actions you gain personal power and complete control over how your life will turn out. If you exhibit the symptoms of "the illness" like a negative mindset and attitude, be sure to remind yourself that you can change your mind and in doing so you can change your life.

It's also important to understand the CWBS is currently evolving as the Drift becomes more diversified. Try and imagine what happens when a white person in the drift decides to change their way of thinking and then convince other white people to do the same. It causes a major disruption in the drift. Think about the disruption, courage and commitment it took from Abraham Lincoln to abolish slavery and convince the American people that it was immoral and unjust.

Obviously there was a lot of resistance but eventually, the CWBS was changed. It wasn't easy and a lot of people were definitely not happy about it but ultimately the drift began to change.

Now imagine what happens when black people actually joined the drift and started floating along the drift with white people. Initially, it was total chaos but due to the commitment, courage, strength and faith of black people the drift was completely disrupted and it changed this country for the better. Now we have people of all races, religions, political affiliations and sexual orientations floating along in a current of diversity and we are creating the CHBS; The Collective Human Belief System and herein lies the reason for my optimism. I personally believe in human evolution and I believe human beings are still evolving. We are evolving in consciousness and understanding and despite our negative mainstream media I fervently believe the future is a lot brighter than what most people believe.

It all begins with you becoming aware of the illness of a negative mindset and attitude and being willing to know there is a cure.

My hope is that you've gained some insights from this chapter that will support you in overcoming "The Illness". The time has come for you to find "The Cure" for this illness so if you're ready, I'll meet you in the next chapter.

Take care.

"If you truly want to change your life, you must first be willing to change your mind."

Donald Altman

LESSON TWO:
The Cure

IF YOU ASK most people "who are you" they will respond by saying things like, my name is Michael and I am a writer, a husband, a father, a Christian, a Democrat, I'm 58 years old and I work for _____ (fill in the blank). So take a moment and answer the question for yourself.

Who are you?

Whether you realize it or not, this is possibly the most important question a person can ask themselves yet very few people are actually willing to ask it. If you are really serious about finding a "cure" for the "illness" it all begins with asking yourself this very important question.

One of your greatest challenges as a human being is to be willing to not attach to societal and cultural labels that try and identify and define who you really are. This can be extremely difficult because most of us create superficial masks that we hide behind and these labels become our identities, which keep us from knowing who we really are.

For example; when I was 23 years old I had climbed the corporate ladder and by society's standards, I was successful. I had the house, the wife and the 2.5 kids, I was able to take vacations and I had excellent credit. On the surface it looked like I had it all. As I look back in retrospect I can see how my life was a complete fake. I was living a lie. Even though I had all the external things society says you're supposed to have to be happy I was absolutely miserable. Of course I didn't recognize this at the time because I was trapped behind a superficial mask. My identity was tied to my accomplishments and I had no idea who I really was. I identified as a husband, a father and a manager but truthfully I had no clue as to who I really was.

When I was 25 I began reading personal development books in an attempt to become a better manager and I ran across a book titled Your Erroneous Zones by Dr. Wayne Dyer. In the book, he shared something that completely changed my perception of myself and it was a statement that put me on the path to self-discovery. This is the quote that would change my life forever and put me on a journey of constant and never-ending improvement that I'm still on today more than 30 something years later.

He said this: "As a human being, you have within you the capacity to do anything any other human being has done. And if it has never been done, you can be the first." I wish I could put into words the impact that quote had on me. I kept reading it over and over again because it touched something deep inside of me that had been lying dormant for a very long time.

As I read the quote something in me shifted. I had this amazing clarity of understanding for the first time of what it meant to be human. As I contemplated the quote I asked myself is the quote applicable to me as a black man? And my heart screamed with a resounding and delightful Yes! Of course, it's applicable to you because you are a human being.

At that moment I stopped viewing myself as just a black man. I saw myself as a man who happened to be black with unlimited potential who could accomplish anything he set his mind to. It was that recognition that has allowed me to far exceed what society says a black male without a high school diploma should be able to accomplish.

Amazingly, I have received a lot of criticism as a black man who identifies himself as a man who happens to be black versus saying I am a black man. I've been accused of being a sellout and denying my ethnicity but in reality, I'm not denying my ethnicity I'm simply affirming my humanity.

Herein lies "The Cure" for Onlyness. To be willing to acknowledge your humanness and discover who you really are.

When you are trapped in the CWBS or the CBBS you will identify with stereotypes and labels that will keep you from knowing who you really are. For example, the CWBS created the label called "minority" which too many men of color accept as their identity. But have you ever really thought about what a minority is? Let's dissect it just a bit to give you a better understanding.

One definition is: "A group having little power or representation relative to other groups within a society."

Let that sink in for a moment. Do you see black people as a group having little power? I don't! I see black people as powerful, courageous and faithful. If you base the word minority on the number of people in this country then obviously we could be defined as a minority because we only make up 13% of the population. But unfortunately, too many black people see being a minority in the context of being powerless and it definitely contributes to the illness of a negative mindset and attitude.

It amazes me how many black people accept this minority label without giving any thought to its meaning. Too many people identify with this label and wear it proudly as a badge of honor. The truth is, it perpetuates a victim and powerless mentality that is definitely a part of the "Illness".

So let's be clear. You are not a minority. This does not mean you are denying your ethnicity. It means you are refusing to accept a label created by the CWBS that will keep you trapped in mediocrity.

So, are you willing to discover who and what you really are? Are you willing to move past CWBS and CBBS labels to uncover the real you?

Since you're still reading I am going to assume you are ready so let's begin with some wisdom from one of my previous books titled - Adversity Is Your Greatest Ally – How To Use Life Challenges To Live The Life Of Your Dreams. (Be sure to add it to your reading list)

I would like for you to take a moment to read the quote below.

"You are more than your thoughts, your body, or your feelings. You are a swirling vortex of limitless potential who is here to shake

things up and create something new that the Universe has never seen."

As you read the quote, what thoughts came to mind? How did you feel after reading it? Did you feel excited? Scared? Confused? Uncertain? What if the quote is true? What if I told you that you are an unlimited being with infinite potential?

Would you believe me?

Unfortunately, most people wouldn't. But the fact that you are reading this book right now tells me that you are not "most people". If you are the type of person who reads a book like this, that tells me that you are open minded, curious, and willing to learn and grow, and therefore it's quite possible that you believe the quote. As a matter of fact, you've probably already agreed with it and are now ready to create something new that the Universe has never seen - so let's just jump right in and get started.

The truth is, there's an overwhelming majority of people who do not believe the quote. They will accept societally-driven labels that define who they are without ever asking themselves deeper questions like "who am I and why am I here?" This chapter is designed to give you some insights on possibly answering those two questions for you. Are you ready to answer those questions for yourself?

As I mentioned earlier, if you ask most people who they are, they will usually respond with answers such as their name, whether they have a family, what they do for a living, if they are a democrat or republican, an African American or Caucasian, a Christian or a Muslim (or are part of a host of other religions), an American or Asian - the list of labels goes on and on. But if you think really deeply about this, these are just titles and labels that we use to try to define who we are. To prove my point, I want you to do a simple test. Walk up to a mirror and ask yourself what you see. Do you see a republican? A Christian? A husband? A manager?

The answer is that you see a human being. The mirror can't lie, it can only reflect that which is placed in front of it. All the titles and labels that you use to define yourself isn't who you are; they are simply titles, labels, and beliefs that you have accepted to define yourself. For example, have you ever known someone who used to be a republican, but then became a democrat? Or someone who was a Christian, who then became a Muslim? Or maybe someone who was pro-life, then became pro-choice? If they looked in the mirror as a republican and then became a democrat what would they see in the mirror? They would see a human being, not a label. Labels are really just beliefs. You are not a label. You are a human being with different beliefs, and although your beliefs may change, you will not.

What you see in the mirror is what you truly are, but it goes a lot deeper than that. *What* you are, is not necessarily *who* you are.

Let me explain in more detail.

What you are is a human being with flesh and bones. This is an undisputable fact. But *who* you are is the divine being that resides within the flesh and bones. Here is another way to look at it - if I stand in front of a mirror and look at myself, I notice that I'm wearing a shirt. So if I say that is "my" shirt, who owns it? I do - it is "my" shirt. Now, I continue to look into the mirror and notice my body. Who is the "me" that owns the body? If this is "my" body, who am I? I would like to suggest that the "me" that owns the body is actually my spirit. Put another way, you are not actually a human being having a spiritual experience - you are a spiritual being having a human experience, and your body is just like the suit of clothes that you are wearing.

If you can wrap your mind around this idea then the original quote that I began with should make more sense to you. The quote said, "You are a swirling vortex of limitless potential who is here to shake things up and create something new that the Universe has never seen." Which simply means that you are a divine spiritual being expressing yourself through human form. You have unique gifts and talents that must be shared with the world if you truly want to live a rewarding and fulfilling life.

So what do you think? Do you believe this? Can you accept that you are much more than your physical body? Can you embrace the idea that you are a divine spiritual being with unlimited potential who is here to shake things up?

Since you're still reading this book that means you're ready to dive deep into who you really are! So let's begin with understanding your divine makeup.

You are actually a three part being which can be described as body, mind, and spirit. You are a spirit, which is housed in a body that has a mind. Your body is like the clothes you are wearing, and your mind is like a tool that you use to help make conscious decisions and to learn new things. They all work in harmony.

As a spiritual being, you have an infinite capacity for learning and creativity. There are absolutely no limits to the number of things you can learn and create. You are only limited by your imagination, and even your imagination is unlimited.

So, let's break down the three parts of your being.

Let's begin with your mind.

It's important that you understand what your mind is and how it works if you truly want to discover who you really are. I'll begin by saying that the mind and the brain are not really the same thing. Your brain is the organ that serves as the center of your nervous system and is responsible for cognitive thinking and memory. In my opinion, it is the most amazing organ in your body, and it works just like a muscle - the more you use it, the stronger it gets.

The mind, however, is separate and distinct from the brain, although they work together. It is almost impossible to truly define the mind. Scientists have been trying to define it in scientific terms for millennia, but unfortunately, there has never been a consensus on exactly what the mind is. Rather than try to argue and define it, I will simply share a definition that I truly resonate with, and it is this definition I will use to explain what I believe the mind does and how it works.

The mind is *"the element of a person that enables them to be aware of the world and their experiences, to think, and to feel; the faculty of consciousness and thought."*

I really like the last part of this definition; *the faculty of consciousness and thought.*

According to Dr. Bruce Lipton, author of the amazing book The

Biology Of Belief, the mind actually has two parts; the conscious mind and the subconscious mind. A great metaphor to explain how it works is an iceberg. If you look at an iceberg in the ocean you will only see a small portion of it above the water, but did you know that in some cases 90% of the iceberg is actually below the surface? This is how the mind works. The top 10% is your conscious mind, and the lower 90% is your subconscious mind. What is really fascinating is that the subconscious mind is actually 1000 times more powerful than the conscious mind when it comes to influencing your behavior.

Dr. Lipton explained it this way;

When we are born, we are completely conscious of all the external stimuli that we interact with. As children, we process primarily through our feelings without judgment or thought about the situation. In other words, we use our hearts, not our minds, to interpret everything around us. Our feelings become the guidepost of our experiences.
During the first 7-10 years of our lives, our subconscious mind works like a video recorder. It simply records all the external events in our lives, and then it begins associating feelings, memories, and beliefs with those events. As we grow older, we begin to form subconscious beliefs about everything we come into contact with. As we form these beliefs we then begin making assumptions about who we are and how we fit into the world. Our prerecorded tapes become our subconscious beliefs about ourselves, and everything we think and do are then filtered through, and influenced by, these prerecorded tapes.

So take a moment to think about your own childhood, especially between when you were born and when you turned seven. What do you remember? Do you remember growing up in a loving, caring home, or was it one filled with violence and dysfunction?

Whether you realize it or not, your childhood has a strong impact on your behavior, even as an adult. If you remember being loved and nurtured as a child, the chances are your subconscious mind is filled with positive beliefs about yourself. In other words, your prerecorded tapes are positive, which in most cases means you will feel good about yourself and have a positive attitude about life. On the other hand, if you remember pain and misery growing up, there is a good chance that your prerecorded tapes about yourself may be negative, which in turn may cause you to create a negative outlook on life.

You can look at the subconscious mind as a big memory bank that stores your beliefs, memories, and life experiences. All your thoughts are instantly processed through your subconscious beliefs. Look at it this way - once your subconscious tapes are programmed during your childhood, every thought and action you have as an adult will be based on the programming you experienced growing up.

I'd like to take this time to share an example from my own life.

I was separated from my mom at the age of six, where I then created a subconscious belief that the people who love you will always leave you. As an adult that may sound irrational, but as a six-year-old, my mother meant the world to me and having her leave me was devastating and emotionally traumatizing.

As a result of this event, I created a subconscious belief that there was something wrong with me that caused my mother to leave. The primary belief I created was that I was unlovable. In order not to feel the shame and abandonment I experienced when my mother left, I created an unconscious strategy that I thought would keep me from feeling pain, and also to keep people in my life from leaving.

That strategy was for me to become a super nice guy in hopes of keeping people around that I cared about. By becoming a super nice guy I put other people's emotional and psychological needs ahead of my own, and I was constantly trying to take care of others before taking care of myself. This is called *co-dependence*, and it was the reason I struggled with relationships earlier in my life.

I didn't realize it as I was growing up, but that single event laid the foundation of how I interacted in all of my relationships as an adult. My subconscious beliefs about myself actually sabotaged my relationships.

I would enter into a relationship where I would be the super nice guy. I would do all the right things that a woman would want in a relationship. I was attentive and respectful, and I had no problems showing affection. I had a great sense of humor and definitely believed in monogamy. On the surface, I appeared to be the perfect guy, but unfortunately, my subconscious beliefs about not being good enough and the deep-seated fear of abandonment kept me from being truly authentic in relationships, which kept me from experiencing true intimacy. No matter how much a woman loved me, that deep-rooted fear I had convinced me that something was wrong with me, which led to the fear that eventually the women in my life would leave.

Based on this subconscious fear, what do you think happened in my relationships? Of course, the women in my life would leave. I created an amazing pattern in all of my relationships, especially after my divorce. I would enter into a relationship and it would last two to three weeks, and then the women would end up saying that they "cared too much" about me to stay in the relationship.

At the time, it made absolutely no sense to me that women would say that. How could you care about someone, but at the same time leave them? After some deep self-introspection and emotional healing, I was able to recognize how my subconscious beliefs had been sabotaging my relationships, and I figured out how to break the pattern (I will explain how I did this in the next chapter).

The point I'm trying to make is how powerful the subconscious mind really is. Remember, the subconscious mind is separate and distinct from your brain - it is the faculty of consciousness and thought.

On the other hand, you have your conscious mind, which could be referred to as your "intellect". The conscious mind is where you store information that you have learned through rigorous study and learning. When you go to school and learn facts, you are using your conscious mind. When you calculate and figure out solutions to most problems, you are also using your conscious mind, but remember what I said about the subconscious mind is 1000 times more powerful than the conscious mind?

Here is an example of how this works.

Imagine that you know someone that has a PhD in astrophysics.

This person is obviously extremely intelligent and has a highly-developed conscious mind. But imagine too that this person has difficulty creating healthy relationships. No matter what they do, they always experience difficulty in relationships. Why do you think this is? They are obviously very smart, and yet they can't figure out how to make relationships work. Why is that?

Well, it's actually pretty simple. On a conscious level, they can read a book about relationships and explain to you intellectually how relationships work, which uses the conscious mind. But their subconscious is 1000 times more powerful than their conscious mind, so when they enter into a relationship, the subconscious beliefs they have about themselves will always override the conscious mind. No matter how many books they read or how smart they are, if they have deeply rooted negative subconscious beliefs about themselves, they will never be able to create healthy relationships.

This is why it is so important to understand how the mind works. No matter how much we may learn on a conscious level, if we aren't willing to look at our subconscious beliefs, we can never truly change our lives. We each have deeply held subconscious beliefs about a wide variety of things and until we become willing to change these subconscious beliefs, we will not be able to overcome our subconscious conditioning.

Let's take a look at some subconscious beliefs that may be sabotaging your life right now.

Are you currently struggling financially and can't figure out why? Well, there is a very good chance that your subconscious beliefs are actually keeping you from being financially secure. If you grew up hearing that money was the root of all evil or that rich people were stuck up and selfish, you may have subconscious beliefs that keep you from making a lot of money, because your subconscious belief might be that money is "bad".

If you're a man and you struggle with relationships, you may have subconscious beliefs that say women only want you for your money or women can't be trusted. This belief will eventually sabotage any new relationship you enter. If you're a woman and struggle with relationships, then it's quite possible that you have subconscious beliefs that say all men are dogs and only want sex. Therefore this belief will keep you from creating true intimacy with men because of your lack of trust. If you happen to be religious, you may have subconscious beliefs that you are a sinner and there is nothing you can do except repent of your sins and hope that God forgives you for being a sinner.

No matter what subconscious beliefs you have, you must understand that it is those subconscious beliefs that are actually the cause of most of the pain, suffering, and lack of experience you have in life. To sum it up, your subconscious beliefs create your reality, so if you aren't happy with any area of your life right now, I can assure you that the main reason is that you have some unconscious belief that is causing you pain and misery.

It is absolutely imperative that you begin examining your deeply held subconscious beliefs if you truly want to change, but rest assured that it *is* possible for you to do so.

Now that you have a deeper understanding of how the subconscious mind works, here's the really good news - when you realize just how powerful the mind really is, you can use it to create anything you want in life.

Have you ever heard this quote: "Whatever the mind can conceive, you can achieve, if you really believe"?

Do you believe it? Is it really possible?

I believe the answer is "yes" and now I would like to share how and why this is possible. So let's go back to the definition I posted earlier: The mind is *"the element of a person that enables them to be aware of the world and their experiences, to think, and to feel; the faculty of consciousness and thought."*

I would like you to focus on *"the faculty of consciousness and thought."*

Here is another way to look at it. Try to imagine there is a Divine Intelligence that permeates the Universe. This Intelligence is actually the Source of all things. It is inherent in all things. It is what keeps the planets aligned and what causes a seed to grow into a flower. It is the same intelligence that causes a bone to heal and the earth to orbit the sun.

There are lots of different names for this Source, but the name does not matter. You can call it God, The Creator, Yahweh, Jehovah, Great Spirit, The Universe, or any other name, but what is most important is that you believe and trust that it is available to you (throughout this book I will simply refer to it as The Source). You do not have to believe in any particular religion or dogma to have access to it, you must simply open your heart and your mind to the truth that it exists. If you accept this truth, then you must accept that your mind is actually connected to The Source. Your mind is like a conduit through which The Source allows divine intelligence to flow to you and through you.

Now you must remember what I said at the beginning. **The mind and the brain are not the same thing.** The brain can only process information that you have provided to it. The brain is not creative - it is not the source of imagination, creativity, or divine ideas. The brain is also not the source of inspiration or insight; these are all functions of the mind, which can also be referred to as the heart, or the center of your being.

Author and spiritual teacher IyanlaVanzantsaid*"The mind is a powerful, creative energy. Everything we think, do and feel begins in the mind. For this reason, we have to address the thoughts, beliefs, judgments, learning's, and perceptions that we hold in our minds."*

The reason the quote "whatever the mind can conceive you can achieve" is true, is because the Source of all things is purely creative and it needs you to co-create with it. So when your mind conceives a divine idea from The Source, which is all-powerful and limitless, you can accomplish it if you're willing to work hand-in-hand with The Source and put forth a whole lot of effort to bring it to fruition.

One of my favorite spiritual teachers is Deepak Chopra. He shared a very powerful quote that really speaks to this truth. He said: "Inherent in every intention and desire are the mechanics for its fulfillment". Put another way, The Source will not give you an idea that you can't accomplish. The Source knows exactly what you're capable of, and will therefore only give you divine ideas that are attainable for you. You wouldn't even have the idea in the first place if you weren't capable of accomplishing it.

As I mentioned previously, the mind is the source of imagination, and therefore it is the key to creating anything you want in life. Let me share a brief story with you to validate my point.

During the darkest period of my life, I was deeply depressed and unsure of how I was ever going to get my life back on track. At the time, I had no money, no job, no relationship, no material possessions, and things seemed pretty hopeless. But the one thing I did have was my imagination, and I began to use it to help me change my situation. Despite that I had absolutely nothing, I began imagining my life getting better. Instead of focusing on all the things I didn't have, I focused my attention on what I did have. I would begin each day counting my blessings for everything that I had, such as my health, my ability to learn, my positive attitude, a few close friends, children who loved me, and the fact that I was even alive.

I began envisioning what my life would be like once I got back on my feet, and I somehow knew that eventually, I would. As I continued to focus on the things that I did have and on the future that I wanted to create, things slowly started to change for me. Eventually I found a job, then I purchased a car, and finally, I was able to get my own apartment. Although this took a couple of years, my point is that I used my imagination to see the things I wanted, and then I worked really hard to get them. It all began in my mind. I had to be willing to use my mind and imagination first before I could create the things I wanted.

As I think back in retrospect I can now see how The Source was actually the source of all of the ideas that I used to put my life back together. It was The Source that would provide me with ideas on where to look for employment, and that gave me the inspiration to remain positive even when I had nothing. It was The Source that gave me the strength and courage to move through all of my life's challenges without giving up and falling victim to despair. It was The Source that encouraged me and helped me to focus on my ultimate destiny, and it didn't allow me to quit.

Even through those difficult times, I held on to my dreams of one day being a successful entrepreneur, writer, and speaker. I had no evidence that I could do these things, I only had the belief and faith that I could. Belief and faith originate in the mind, and I now recognize that each of these originates from The Source.

And now here I am, some twenty years later doing exactly what I imagined I would be doing. All because I chose to believe that whatever the mind can conceive, you can achieve.

It's important that you understand I am no different than you are. I am a divine spiritual being with direct access to The Source, and so are you. You have a mind and direct access to The Source. There is nothing you cannot accomplish if you choose to access your divinity, but it is up to you to go a little deeper and figure out what negative subconscious beliefs you may have about yourself and change them. It is your responsibility to learn more about your mind and begin using it to create the life you deserve.

So, now let's talk about your body.

It is my belief that the most amazing thing on this planet is the human body. I do not believe that there is anything more miraculous. Although most people take their bodies for granted, I believe it is the greatest gift that The Source provided us with. I mentioned earlier that the body is simply a suit of clothing that your spirit wears, so I must admit that The Source knew exactly what it was doing when it created the human body.

Of course, everyone is aware of their own physical body, but did you know that you also have an emotional or energetic body?

If you accept the fact that you are a spiritual being, then it makes it easier to grasp how the emotional/energetic body works.

Think of it this way;

Imagine that you have an opening in the top of your skull, and there is a pipe that goes from the top of your skull to the bottom of your belly. This pipe flows with energy that comes directly from The Source; this energy is your life force, and it permeates your entire being. When you are born, the pipe is completely open and it allows Source energy to flow through you easily. This energy causes you to feel alive and connected to life. This energy is then converted into feelings, which is the spirit's way of communicating with the body. There are primarily four energies that move throughout the energetic body; joy, anger, sadness, and fear.

As a child, whenever you experienced one of these feelings you acted appropriately and expressed the feeling through an emotion. For example, if you felt sad you would cry; if you felt angry you would scream or lash out; if you felt joy you would smile and laugh; and if you felt fear you would close off or retreat. As long as you expressed the feeling appropriately, then the energetic pipe stayed open and clear and your life force energy continues to flow through you.

As you grow older, your parents or family members begin conditioning you to believe that expressing them was wrong, so what happens is you begin to repress and suppress your feelings, and each time you do you begin to create little energy blocks in the pipe. It's like building up plaque in your arteries. The more you suppress your feelings, the more the energetic pipe clogs up, and before you know it the pipe is completely closed and you are cut off from your life force. When this happens you lose your sense of aliveness, because the divine flow of energy has been cut off. Once the flow of energy has been cut off and we have been disconnected from The Source, we then learn to process everything through our conscious mind or intellect, and we become very rational and analytical. In other words, we try to rely on our brains instead of our minds and hearts.

The bad news is the energetic body works like the subconscious mind. We may not be aware of it, but our repressed emotions cause us to act out irrationally sometimes because we are completely unconscious of the pain we may be carrying. Here is a good example. Have you ever met someone or known someone who is always angry? No matter what is going, on this person is angry and negative, and they usually aren't that pleasant to be around. They get angry and upset at the slightest provocation, and no matter what you say or do they will have a negative response to just about everything. Do you know anyone like that? Are *you* like that?

Why do you think this person acts this way? It's because they have trapped emotional energy in their emotional body, and until they learn how to release it, they will always act out of anger.

On the flip side of that, maybe you know someone who always pretends to be happy. They are the "people pleasing" types that always seek approval and they pretend that everything is always okay. The only emotion they express is happiness, but unfortunately, they are completely sad and emotionally bankrupt inside. A person like this usually has trapped anger, fear, or sadness in their emotional bodies, and rather than feel these emotions they hide behind being happy all of the time.

When we have repressed or suppressed emotions they can sabotage all areas of our lives. As long as we feel and release our feelings appropriately, the life force can move through us, but as we shut down the flow, we create a disconnection from The Source and it leads to all sorts of problems in our lives.

It's important that you take care of both of your bodies - your physical body and your emotional one. You take care of the physical body by eating the right foods and exercising, and you take care of the emotional body by investing in some emotional healing work that allows you to release any repressed energy that is trapped in your emotional body. I will share some tips on how to do this in the next chapter.

Now that you have a better understanding of how the mind and the body works together, it's time to fully understand who you really are.

Every major religion promotes a very simple and profound truth. There is a Source through which all things are created. It does not matter which religion you follow, as long as you accept this simple fact. This Source is the Divine Intelligence that created and is still creating the Universe, and you have unlimited access to this Source. As a human being, you are a divine expression of this Source, which means that you can co-create anything your heart desires with this Source.

Think of it this way - if you look at the ocean, you will see a powerful, beautiful, and seemingly infinite body of water. If you walk up to the ocean and scoop up a small cup of it, what you will have in the cup is ocean. But the cup of ocean could never be the ocean in its totality, so therefore it is a divine expression of the ocean. This expression is no different than the ocean; as a matter of fact, it contains all of the same qualities, characteristics, and attributes of the ocean. In fact, it is the ocean in an individualized expression. As long as the expression of the ocean stays connected to the ocean it will thrive and express exactly the way the ocean does. But if the ocean in the cup is separated from the ocean, eventually it will dry up and no longer exist as that unique expression.

The Source is just like the ocean. You are an individual expression of the Source. You have all of the same qualities, characteristics, and attributes as the Source. You are no different than The Source. As long as you stay connected to The Source, you can co-create with it, and since The Source is infinite, so are you.

Do not buy into societal labels and constructs that will convince you that there is something wrong with you. Disregard all labels and titles and come to the understanding that you are a divine spiritual being with unlimited potential, and the only thing that can keep you from accomplishing anything is yourself. This includes letting go of the attachment to your ethnic identity. You should definitely be proud of your ethnic heritage, whatever it may be, but you must understand that your spiritual nature has nothing to do with skin color or nationality. The Source transcends race, and therefore so do you if you choose to accept who and what you truly are.

Titles and labels will only hold you back, but accepting the truth of your being will definitely set you free. Remember that you are a three part being - Spirit, Mind, and Body - that is connected to The Source, and you can therefore co-create anything your heart desires.

I would like to close this chapter with something for you to think about.

I would like for you to think about a snowflake.

If you look at snowflakes falling from the sky, it appears that they are all the same. They all have the same color, texture, and smell.

They are all composed of the same stuff, and they all come from the same source. But if you look under a microscope, every snowflake is completely different. No two snowflakes are alike. Just imagine – out of the billions of snowflakes that fall from the sky, none of them are the same.

The truth is, you are just like the snowflake. Out of the 7 billion human beings on the planet, there is only one you. When it comes to human beings, The Source never replicates itself. You are a divine, unique individual expression of The Source, and it is your responsibility to accept this fact.

Your job is to come to this understanding and to recognize that you have unlimited potential, and you have been given some unique gifts and talents that are yours alone - and your job is to share them with the world. This is the reason that the quote I shared at the beginning of the chapter is so important. It states a divine truth, and I hope that you will take it to heart and accept it as *your* truth.

So I will leave you with that quote, and I hope that you will embrace it and accept the truth that it shares.

> *"You are more than your thoughts, your body, or your feelings. You are a swirling vortex of limitless potential who is here to shake things up and create something new that the Universe has never seen."*

Dr. Richard Bartlett

To raise new questions, new possibilities, to regard old problems from a new angle, requires creative imagination and marks a real advance in science.

Albert Einstein

LESSON THREE:
Embrace Science

FROM A VERY early age, I have always had a fascination with science. I have always loved figuring out how things work and learning why people are the way they are. When I was in the 3rd grade I had a favorite science teacher named Ms. Newman who encouraged me to question everything and she instilled in me a deep love for learning.

I remember a question I asked her what was the foundation for my love of psychology and personal development. We had a new student join our class who was Asian. This was back in the 60's and it was the first time I had met someone from Japan. After class, I went up to my teacher and I asked her why a Japanese child born in America didn't speak Japanese. My 3rd-grade mind couldn't wrap around why my new classmate didn't speak Japanese. I remember her trying to explain to me that language was a learned behavior but I still couldn't fully understand why. Ever since asking that question I have had a deep curiosity about human behavior.

My curiosity has been instrumental in me having an open mind and being willing to learn new things. It was this open mind that did not allow me to accept some of the stereotypes and illusions the CWBS and the CBBS tried to get me to believe. During the civil rights movement of the 60's I questioned why there was segregation and why black people and white people appeared to dislike each other. I trusted my own intuition and learned to accept people for who they were and not the color of their skin. I was never afraid to go over to the side of the cafeteria where the white kids sat because I had a crush on this girl and I didn't care she was white. I was attacked from both sides but it didn't matter. I didn't see her as a white girl, I simply saw her as pretty and I really liked her.

As I grew older I maintained my curiosity and open-mindedness and I thought about Mrs. Newman often. She instilled my love for science and her caring and attentive personality left an indelible mark on my heart and she will always have a special place there.

Currently, my three favorite scientists are Albert Einstein, Joe Dispenza, and Neale Degrasse Tyson. I love Albert Einstein for his brilliant mind and his philosophical view of the world.

I love how Joe combines hard science with spiritual insights and his meditations are absolutely divine and heart opening.

I love Neal because of his intelligence and sense of humor. The fact that Neale happens to be black inspires me and challenges me to think objectively about this amazing Universe we live in and to be willing to question reality and my place in it.

I love how Neale shatters the stereotype that black men are less intelligent and he does it without making race an issue. He simply shares his brilliance and expresses his deepest truth and wisdom. One of my favorite quotes from him is: *"Everything we do, every thought we've ever had, is produced by the human brain. But exactly how it operates remains one of the biggest unsolved mysteries, and it seems the more we probe its secrets, the more surprises we find."*

How our brains and mind work is definitely one of the great mysteries of the Universe. It is important for us as black men to understand how our brains and our minds work and to be willing to allow science to help us understand them as much as possible. My experience has taught me that too many times we have relied on religion to try and explain our behavior when in reality, science can teach us a lot more than religion can when it comes to our brains and our minds.

Psychology can be defined as the science of the mind. It allows us to understand why we do what we do and it can provide a roadmap to human behavior. Unfortunately, the CBBS has generally promoted religion over psychology. I remember going to church after my divorce, bankruptcy and foreclosure to try and alleviate some of the emotional

Lesson Three: Embrace Science

pain I was in and when I asked the minister for some advice, his answer was to simply pray about it. From that moment on I stopped believing in God and decided I would figure out how to heal myself through science and psychology.

As a result, I read literally hundreds of books on psychology, philosophy, and personal development, and eventually, I was able to rebuild my life. Of course, it took a lot more than just reading books. I went to therapy, engaged in workshops and seminars and listened to hours upon hours of personal development audio programs. It has been a 30-year journey for me but it all culminated into me being completely happy with myself and my life and now I'm committed to sharing the lessons I've learned with others to support them on their journey to wholeness.

As I reflect back on my journey, the most important lesson I learned was the importance of dealing with childhood trauma. Within the CBBS there is a resistance to talk about the impact trauma has on our well-being. I have come to know that religion seldom heals emotional and psychological trauma. As a matter of fact, religion can actually exacerbate emotional trauma. When a religion promotes the idea that we are born sinners that must repent of our sins it perpetuates the idea that we are defective and unlovable and it destroys our self-esteem. Therefore I believe it is important to embrace science in a way that gives us a better understanding of our behavior so we can make the necessary changes and adjustments in our psyches to ensure we are psychologically healthy and whole.

With that being said, I want to talk about the importance of making peace with your past. I have come to believe there is nothing more important than dealing with childhood trauma. As a human being, we all experience different levels of trauma and different people deal with trauma in different ways. But it is important to recognize that our childhood definitely has an impact on our adult lives and if we aren't willing to examine childhood trauma it will sabotage our lives as adults.

Here is another excerpt from my book Adversity Is Your Greatest Ally that will provide you with some insights in making peace with your past and moving past childhood trauma.

When I became involved with personal development programs back in 1990 I was really drawn into the teaching of the power of positive thinking. I had always been an optimistic person, so it was a natural progression for me to really embrace what a lot of the motivational speakers were preaching. Their message was to always be positive and look at the bright side of things. It was this positive thinking that allowed me to deal with the multiplicity of challenges I was dealing with at the time. If not for my positive thinking, I'm sure that I would have fallen into a deep abyss of despair and depression, which may have ultimately ended up with my demise.

But I embraced the positive thinking mantra and made a commitment to always think positive. Without question, this way of thinking has positively impacted my life, but there was a negative side of positive thinking that I want to share, to shed some light on why positive thinking sometimes doesn't work and can also be detrimental to your life.

The biggest lesson I learned about the detrimental effects of positive thinking occurred while I was basically homeless. I had a friend that allowed me to stay at her house for a while until I could find a place of my own. During that time I was searching for employment and doing everything I could to get back on my feet. I didn't own a car and she would sometimes let me borrow hers to look for employment. She was an absolute angel whom I am forever indebted to for her generosity, caring, and friendship.

One evening my friend came home and asked me how my day went. I told her about the rejections I had received while trying to find a job, and I told her that I was still optimistic that I would find a job soon.

She then looked at me with a caring compassionate heart and she asked how I was really doing. The conversation went something like this:

> Her: *Michael, tell me how you're really doing. How are you feeling right now?*

Lesson Three: Embrace Science

Me: *I'm doing great! Although I didn't find a job I'm confident that I will soon and I will be able to get back on my feet.*

Her: *But Michael, you didn't answer my question. How are you feeling right now? In this very moment, how do you feel?*

Me: *I told you I'm doing great. I know the Universe is going to support me and help me find a job so I'm excited and happy about my future.*

Her: *Michael, I think that's bullshit! You keep saying you're doing great but the truth is you aren't. Right now your life is a mess and you're unwilling to be completely honest with yourself about how you really feel. I believe in you and have faith in you that you will get your life on track, but until you are able to be completely honest with yourself about how you feel, not what you think, you really won't be able to change. I personally think that you are in denial and you are hiding behind your positive thinking and denying how you really feel. Can you tell me right now exactly what you're feeling?*

Me: *I told you, I'm doing great. I've got some challenges to deal with but I keep telling you that I'll deal with them. What more do you want me to say?*

Her: *I want you to share your feelings with me. Tell me what's going on inside you. Not what's in your head, but what's in your heart. How do you feel?*

Me: *I don't really understand what you're asking. I keep telling you that I'm fine. What else can I say?*

Her: *So Michael, answer this question, how does it make you feel to not be able to have your own home and have to rely on other people? Does it make you sad? Does it make you angry?*

How did you feel when you were rejected for the jobs you applied for today? Were you upset? Were you disappointed? Were you afraid?

Or how does it make you feel when you know you can't see your kids because you don't have transportation or money to visit them? Doesn't that make you feel sad?

Do you see what I mean now? I want you to share your emotions with me. I want you to express your feelings. Can you do that?

    Me: *I'm not sure.*

    Her: *Michael, you and I have been through a lot together as friends. I love how you are able to be optimistic and positive, and I love how you can find the good in all situations. But the truth is you aren't connected to your emotions and you hide behind being positive and intellectual. You are so stuck in your head that you can't feel from your heart.*

    You are my friend and I love you. I will never judge you or reject you. I'm not asking anything from you except your willingness to be authentic and real with me. Can you do that? Can you share yourself with me in that way?

After listening to her for a moment I started to allow myself to feel. I really started looking closer at myself for what emotions were present, and all of a sudden I knew what she meant. At that moment I felt my heart beginning to surrender and I began to speak.

    Me: *I understand what you mean now. If I'm completely honest I feel sad and afraid. I'm sad because I feel like less than a man because I have to rely on you to take care of me. I feel afraid that I'm not going to be able to find a job and ultimately you will have to kick me out on the streets and I'm not sure what I will do.*

    Her: *That's what I'm talking about. Keep sharing. Tell me more about how you feel.*

    Me: *I really feel like a failure right now. I worked so hard to build my perfect life, only to have it come crashing down on me. I've lost everything. I lost my wife, my kids, my home, my job, and my self-esteem. I feel lonely and sad right now.*

All of a sudden my friend walks over and begins to hug me. She takes me in her arms and tells me that everything is going to be okay. She assures me that it is okay to share what I'm feeling and that it does not make me less of a man to do so. As she continued to hold me in her warm embrace, I continued to share how I was feeling. I allowed all the trapped emotions to come out and the tears began to flow. I found myself releasing years of repressed pain, sadness, and disappointment, and the emotions just began to pour out of me through my tears. Although it was extremely painful, it was also therapeutic. Allowing myself to feel and express those emotions was extremely healing and cathartic. Before long my tears of sadness and pain turned to tears of joy, as I recognized just how much my friend cared about me and how much love I was feeling from her at that moment.

> Me: *I am so glad we are having this conversation because I'm really tired of pretending that everything is okay. I have been hiding behind this new-age spiritual positive thinking mask for so long I haven't allowed myself just to feel my emotions. I guess there was a part of me that believed if I shared the negative things in my life it meant that I didn't have faith that it would get better. But now I realize this isn't true. Just because I may be feeling sad or afraid does not mean that I've lost faith, it just means that I'm human and I have feelings and I should always be aware of, and true to, those feelings.*
>
> Her: *The key to happiness is being in touch with how you truly feel and being able to express whatever you feel openly and honestly. Feelings are neither good nor bad, they just are. Emotions are just energy in motion which really is a human being's way of receiving internal feedback and then expressing your internal response to external stimuli. In reality, our emotions are our internal guidance system that keeps us in touch with our humanness.*
>
> *Now that we've had this conversation, I hope that you will be able to speak with me openly and honestly about how you really feel, and you should know that negativity isn't necessarily a bad thing. If you focus on it too much it can make matters worse, but the key is to always be honest with how you really feel, no matter what situation you may be in. I accept you unconditionally as a friend and I'm going to be here for you even when things are tough. You don't have to impress me with your optimism and intellect because I accept you for who you are, not what you do. Do you understand?*
>
> Me: *I really do. This experience has really been good for me and it has opened my eyes to the fact that I still have some healing*

and some growing to do. Thank you so much for seeing through my positive mask and challenging me to take it off. I promise that I will do my best to be as open and as honest as I possibly can when I'm speaking with you. Thank you so much for being my friend. I love you!

After that conversation, I had to carry out some deep soul searching to figure out exactly why it was so difficult for me to initially express my feelings to my friend. As I contemplated our conversation I was able to see a pattern in my life that I had been using for a very long time. I always used positivity as a way of not expressing my true feelings to others, and I always sought other people's approval to feel good about myself.

I knew that I wanted to break this pattern, and I decided that I would figure out what steps I needed to take to do so.

I decided to talk to my friend to see if she could begin shedding some light on my behavior. She informed me that one of the reasons why I may have had so much difficulty expressing my feelings could have been the result of some childhood trauma. She shared her own experience about going to therapy to deal with some issues from her childhood, and she suggested that I consider therapy that may help me deal with my issues.

She then said something that really stood out for me. It was a statement that was so powerful it literally caused me to rethink everything I had learned in the personal development arena. She looked at me and said; "I don't care how positive you are, how many books you read, or how many seminars you go to. Until you make peace with your past you will never truly be happy."

It was this statement that challenged me to thoroughly examine my entire philosophy on personal development.

I then realized that all the motivational seminars and books I had read did not help me make peace with my past, so I decided to make it the number one priority in my life. I intuitively knew that making peace with my past was the missing link to finding true happiness.

Lesson Three: Embrace Science

I recently ran across a quote by author and spiritual teacher IyanlaVanzant that fully embodies why making peace with your past is so important. This powerful quote holds the key to your happiness and I suggest that you read it slowly (and several times) and intently so that you fully grasp the implications of its message.

> *"Until you heal the wounds of your past, you are going to bleed. You can bandage the bleeding with food, with alcohol, with drugs, with work, with cigarettes, with sex; but eventually, it will all ooze through and stain your life. You must find the strength to open the wounds, stick your hands inside, pull out the core of the pain that is holding you in your past, the memories, and make peace with them."*

Herein lies the key to your happiness. What I've learned over the last twenty years is that we must be willing to heal our hearts and make peace with our past if we truly want to be happy. We can read all the self-help books in the world and listen to audio programs or go to seminars with motivational speakers, but if we fail to carry out our healing work we will unconsciously sabotage our lives and ultimately keep ourselves from being completely happy.

Amazingly there are some people who do not believe that their childhood can actually have an adverse effect on their adult lives. Have you ever heard someone say that their parents used to beat them when they were little, yet they still turned out okay? This statement is a defense mechanism that keeps people trapped in their pain and they will rationalize that their traumatic childhoods had no effect on them whatsoever. The truth is, if you remember being beaten as a child and you have not done any healing work, I can assure you that it will have an effect on your life today.

If you read the preceding chapter and the part about the subconscious mind, this should make sense to you. There are negative beliefs that you may have stored about yourself that could be causing you to unconsciously sabotage your life. This can show up as failed relationships, anxiety, depression, anger issues, or an overall feeling that something is simply missing from your life.

The Cure For Onlyness

The key to making peace with your past lies in your willingness to heal any emotional scars that you may be carrying from your childhood. Healing your heart is the key to making peace with your past. Psychologists will tell you that at their core, all addictions have an unresolved emotional conflict, which simply means that there are emotional wounds that need to be healed.

What IyanlaVanzant meant when she said *"You must find the strength to open the wounds, stick your hands inside, pull out the core of the pain that is holding you in your past, the memories, and make peace with them"* is that it is your responsibility to look within your own heart and find where the pain is, and be willing to heal that pain.

There is a powerful scene in the movie Star Wars, in which Luke Skywalker is being trained by the Master Teacher Yoda. In the scene, Yoda tells Luke that he must enter into a dark cave to face his demons and ultimately become a Jedi Knight. As Luke begins to look into the cave, he turns to Yoda and asks: "What's in the cave." To which Yoda replies; "Only what you take with you." As Luke goes into the cave he is confronted by his nemesis, Darth Vader. Darth Vader is the antagonist in the movie who embraces "The Dark Side." As Darth Vader approaches, Luke pulls out his Light Saber and begins fighting with him. After a brief battle, Luke chops off Darth Vader's head and it appears that he has defeated the bad guy. As Luke looks at the severed head, smoke suddenly issues from the helmet Vader is wearing. As the smoke clears, Luke looks inside the helmet and sees his own face.

The symbolism of this scene speaks directly to the importance of making peace with your past. Luke Skywalker represents the good in every human being, and his training with the Master represents the importance of having teachers to guide us on our personal growth journeys to find the good that is within us. The dark cave represents your subconscious mind that stores all of your erroneous negative beliefs about yourself. It is the place where fear resides, and we must be willing to enter the cave if we truly want to make peace with our past and not live in fear.

Darth Vader represents the parts of ourselves that we are sometimes afraid to look at. He symbolizes our shadows, which are the parts

Lesson Three: Embrace Science

of ourselves that we sometimes hide, suppress, or deny. The battle represents the struggle that we must go through in order to shed light on the dark places in our minds and hearts that keep us from expressing who we really are. Cutting off Darth Vader's head and then Luke seeing his own face represents facing our demons within, and then allowing the dark parts of ourselves to die so that we can be resurrected into who we truly are.

The key is to remember what Yoda said about what's in the cave. "Only what you take with you." This means that the darkness we perceive is only in our minds. The so called darkness is simply erroneous beliefs that we hold about ourselves, and when we become courageous enough to face our own inner darkness, that part of us dies and the real part of us awakens.

There are some people who prescribe to the idea that you do not have to address your childhood wounds in order to be successful and happy. They believe that it does not do any good to "dig up" old hurts. I completely disagree with this way of thinking. I believe that it is absolutely imperative that you are willing to look at the dark events in your life, and are willing to shed light on them. If you are unwilling to do so, those dark places will eventually sabotage your happiness.

There is a term called "spiritual bypassing", which means a person refuses to heal their inner wounds because they have accepted a specific religious teaching that says that God can heal you. I used to hold that belief. At one time I thought that if I prayed enough and followed religious dogma and doctrine, then I would eventually become happy. My own experience has taught me otherwise. It wasn't until I became courageous enough to make peace with my past and deal with some childhood trauma that I was able to heal my heart and become genuinely happy.

When I decided that I wanted to heal my wounds I was introduced to a man named John Bradshaw who facilitated a program called Healing Your Inner Child. In one of his workshops, I learned how my abusive childhood was at the core of all the dysfunction in my life. I learned that I had abandonment issues as a result of being separated from my mom when I was six years old, and I also learned that for the majority of my adult life I was driven by a deep sense of shame. It was my internal feelings of shame that drove me to be successful. I worked really hard to gain other people's approval because deep down I didn't feel worthy.

Although it was extremely difficult, I made the choice to heal my heart and make peace with my past. I took Iyanla's advice and found the strength to open my wounds and stick my hands inside and pull out the core of my pain that was keeping me trapped in my past - and I made peace with them.

As a result of doing this work, I can honestly admit in this very moment I am happier today than I've ever been in my life. It definitely wasn't easy, but I can assure you that it was worth it.

I hope that you will take some time and really think about what I've just shared. Do not make the same mistakes that I did in thinking that being positive will solve all of your problems. Of course, there is absolutely nothing wrong with being positive, and I am still a huge advocate of positive thinking. The key is to make sure that you aren't hiding behind positivity because of some unresolved emotional pain the way I did.

If you are committed to making peace with your past and are looking for some ways to do so, let me make a few suggestions for you to consider. First of all, I think it's really important that you are willing to seek support if needed. I realize that there is a lot of negative stigmas attached in seeking support, but that is a sign of strength, not weakness, when you choose to seek help.

Here are a few things for you to consider if you are truly ready to make peace with your past.

1. Therapy

There is nothing wrong with seeking out a good therapist to support you in dealing with any emotional challenges you may be facing. Our society has conditioned us to believe that we are supposed to carry the weight of the world on our shoulders and not seek support, but this simply isn't true. We all need support at one time or another, so if you've been looking for ways to help you make peace with your past, a good therapist may be exactly what you need.

I would like to share an article I wrote a while ago that shares my first experience with therapy. My hope is that it will give you some insight on how difficult and challenging it might be, but also to inspire you to take the first step if you think you will benefit from therapy. The article is titled "Men's Emotional Healing."

In 1989 I had a series of traumatic experiences that were beginning to take their toll. My divorce and separation from my kids were extremely painful and had begun to negatively impact my life. I had slipped into a deep state of depression and was barely able to function on a daily basis. As my depression deepened I went into isolation, where I literally shut myself off from the outside world.

Although I was able to go to work and function in that capacity, I was completely disconnected from any social settings. I was not dating, and I did not socialize with my friends. I also had difficulty sleeping. I would rarely eat and I had begun to lose weight, which was rare for me, being a former personal trainer that took excellent care of my physical body. After several months I began to have fleeting thoughts of suicide, and it appeared that my situation was hopeless. In an effort to alleviate some of the pain, I begin to read books dealing with depression.

As I read them I could see myself in some of the stories. I definitely had all of the symptoms of depression, and I knew that I had to deal with it head on if I ever wanted to get my life back on track. After reading several books I realized that I was still deeply depressed and had not really begun to deal with the issues that were causing my depression. Instinctively I knew that I needed help, and I decided that I would seek therapy.

After making the decision to get help, another series of challenges surfaced. First of all, how was I going to find a therapist? How would I know which one to choose? What if the therapist couldn't help me? Would I be able to change? Could therapy "fix" me? What about the money to pay for it? I was completely broke and definitely couldn't pay someone to listen to my problems. What was I going to do? These were just a few of the questions that were going through my mind.

My greatest fear was wondering what would happen if my employees found out. As a manager, I was considered the leader and I definitely didn't want to appear weak in front of my co-workers. I believed that I needed to keep this a secret so that I would not lose the respect of my employees. In addition, I did not want my superiors to know because I thought I might lose my job if they found out.

After a few months of agonizing over these questions, I knew that I had to take the chance and try therapy. I didn't have any other choice. It was seek help or die - there was no gray area. I decided that I definitely wanted to live, and I somehow gained the courage to seek a therapist.

My first attempt at therapy did not go well. I walked into the therapist's office and pretended that I was seeking information for a friend. I'm sure the people there knew this was a lie, but they allowed me to walk out with some of their brochures and a phone number to their suicide hotline.

To be honest, I was absolutely terrified. But although I was scared, deep down I knew that I would have to gain the courage to try again. I waited for a few days and tried a different therapist office. This time I had a completely different result.

As I walked into the office I believe the receptionist picked up on my fear. I began asking her questions about depression and whether or not they had any books that I could read. All of a sudden a therapist walked out and began asking me questions. "May I help you?" she asked. "Not really, I'm just looking for a little information about depression." "Are you depressed?" "I'm not really sure," I answered. "Why don't you come inside and let's talk a little. Is that alright?" "I guess so."

As I followed her into her office it felt as if my heart was going to jump out of my chest. I was so nervous and afraid that I was literally dripping with sweat. She obviously picked up on this and began to put my mind at ease.

"*What is your name?*"
"*Michael.*"
"*Well Michael, I can sense that you are a little nervous, so let*

Lesson Three: Embrace Science

me start by asking what I can do to help you. Is there anything I can do for you?"

"Well maybe. I have been doing some research about depression and I think I'm depressed, but I'm really not sure."

"Do you feel depressed?"

"Based on what I've read so far I think I am. But to be completely honest I'm not sure I know exactly what depression is supposed to feel like. Does that make any sense to you?"

"It makes a lot of sense to me. Unfortunately most men do not recognize how they feel. Men have been conditioned to disconnect from their emotions and that makes it extremely difficult for them to express how they really feel. Most men will tell you what they think, but they usually do not know how they feel. You apparently fit into this category."

"I'm not sure if I really understand what you're saying, but a part of me thinks that you're right."

"You just validated the point I made. You are currently speaking from an intellectual perspective, instead of an emotional one. It sounds as if you are disconnected from your emotions."

"Let's assume that you're right. If I am disconnected from my emotions, how do I get reconnected? Do you have any books on how to do this?

"Unfortunately you cannot reconnect to your emotions by reading books. In order for you to reconnect you have to relearn how to feel. This can be accomplished through therapy with me or any trained therapist."

"I really don't understand what you mean. But if I decide to relearn how to feel how long will it take?"

"I really can't answer that question. It's really up to you and how committed you are to doing the work."

"What do you mean doing the work? What kind of work is involved?"

"In the therapeutic community, we use the word 'work' because it takes a considerable amount of effort to heal yourself so that you can reconnect with your emotions. Doing the work means that you

become willing to open yourself up on an emotional level. This can be quite difficult at times."

"Well, I believe I'm ready. I'm really tired of being alone and I definitely want to experience some fun in my life again. I think I can do this, so how much will it cost?"

"I operate on a sliding scale based on your ability to pay. The most important thing is for you to make the commitment to yourself to heal and we can address the money issue at a later date. Are you ready to begin? Let's set up a date and time for you to begin your healing."

"I just wanted to thank you for being so nice and understanding. The truth is I was about to run out of your office before you showed up. Now I am really glad that I came because I really believe that you can help me."

"That is a great attitude to have. I'm glad that you trust me enough to work with you. Just remember that I can guide you, but you must be willing to do the work. As long as you believe that you can heal I can assure you that you will. Just stay committed and trust the process and you will be just fine. The truth is you have already done the hard part by showing up today. It takes an incredible amount of courage to be here and I'm proud of you for taking the first step."

As I left the therapist's office that day I knew I had just taken the biggest step of my life. I didn't know what to expect, but I knew I was willing to do whatever it took to heal my emotions and relearn how to feel. I became committed to my own healing, and I can now say that I'm emotionally healed and connected to my authentic self.

As the therapist mentioned, it wasn't easy, but it was definitely possible. It has been one of the most challenging, yet most fulfilling, journeys of my life.

I cannot put into words the joy I feel on a regular basis as a result of carrying out my emotional work. My relationships now work, my creativity and sense of reverence is enhanced, my love of nature has been rekindled, and my professional life is rewarding and fulfilling.

Lesson Three: Embrace Science

I took the road less traveled and it has made all the difference in the world for me.

I wanted to share this story because there is such a negative stigma about men and therapy that I believe it's time for a new conversation. In this new conversation, men will recognize the importance of healing their emotions and they will put forth the effort to do their healing work.

When we learn to support each other in our growth we can remove the fear and stigma of being emotionally vulnerable, which will ultimately result in us being happier human beings. I personally believe that this is the most important work men can participate in, and we must begin supporting each other through this process.

If we gain the courage to do this work, we will see a decline in domestic violence, child abuse, alcoholism, and random acts of violence. The time has come for a new conversation about our emotional healing.

Are you willing to join in the conversation?

So the first step in making peace with your past is to make sure that you do some emotional healing work. It may be in the form of therapy, but it could also be through support groups like AA or even workshops such as Landmark Education - landmarkeducation.com.

The key is to become 100% committed to healing your heart and making peace with your past. Once you commit and then take action I can assure you that you will begin to feel better about your life, and it will definitely get easier. It won't be an easy process, but I promise you it will be worth it.

2. Workshops/Seminars/Webinars

The second thing I recommend you do is to be willing to participate in personal development seminars. If you have never done anything like this before, you're simply going to have to trust me. There are countless seminars available that can support you in making peace with your past. There are one day seminars, three day retreats, online webinars, and a wide variety of others that can assist you along your journey. Here are just a few that I have found extremely helpful.

If you are male, I highly recommend a three-day workshop called The New Warrior Training Adventure. It is carried out by an organization called The Mankind Project, and without question, it is one of the most transformational experiences you will ever encounter.

You can find out more about them at: **mankindproject.org**.

There are several organizations that offer inner-child healing workshops around the country. I suggest that you research online for inner child work and find a resource in your area. You will simply have to trust yourself and find one that feels right for you. You can begin by reading some books by John Bradshaw if you aren't comfortable attending the workshops. Two of my favorites are *Healing The Shame That Binds You* and *Homecoming*. I highly recommend that you pick up a copy of both.

The key is to become 100% committed to making peace with your past. You have to want it more than anything. You have to listen to that still small voice within you that is calling you to do this work. It's all up to you!

I am absolutely convinced that making peace with your past is a surefire way to achieve true freedom and happiness. As I've mentioned before, it won't be easy, but it will definitely be worth it. If you commit to doing this I can promise you that you will experience deep inner peace, less anxiety, no more depression, a deeper sense of passion and purpose, and a deep inner knowing that you can create the life of your dreams.

Isn't that what you really want - a more rewarding and fulfilling life experience? If the answer is yes, begin by making peace with your past and I can assure you that you will have everything you need to do so.

I would like to close this chapter with a quote from the Dalai Lama. He was once asked what he found most fascinating about human beings, and this is the answer he gave:

"Man sacrifices his health in order to make money. Then he sacrifices money to recuperate his health. And then he is so anxious about the future that he does not enjoy the present moment. As a

result, he does not live in the present or the future, he lives as if he is never going to die, and then he dies having never truly lived."

Make sure you do not make this mistake. If you make peace with your past it will give you lots of reasons to make sure that your life is well lived and that you have absolutely no regrets. Do not die with your music still in you. Learn to sing your song so that the whole world hears you, and you will experience joy that defies human understanding.

Live your life out loud!
You can do this!

"Once upon a time black male "cool" was defined by the ways in which black men confronted hardships of life without allowing their spirits to be ravaged. They took the pain of it and used it alchemically to turn the pain into gold. That burning process required high heat. Black male cool was defined by the ability to withstand the heat and remain centered. It was defined by black male willingness to confront reality, to face the truth, and bear it not by adopting a false pose of cool while feeding on fantasy; not by black male denial or by assuming a "poor me" victim identity. It was defined by individual black males daring to self-define rather than be defined by others."

— Bell Hooks,
We Real Cool:
Black Men and Masculinity

LESSON FOUR:
Masculinity

For the past 24 years, I have been speaking and writing about the changing roles of manhood and masculinity. When I first began writing, there were very few resources for men who were interested in shifting the paradigm of masculinity and usher in a new paradigm that supported men in becoming genuinely happy with their lives. Rarer still were books written by men of color who were talking about how the current paradigm of masculinity was no longer sustainable. Now there are countless books and experts of all ethnicities having this conversation, which fills me with optimism about the future for men.

It is my belief the greatest challenge facing our world today is to redefine masculinity and to support men in creating new ways of being and relating as a man. This is a shift in cultural conditioning, which transcends ethnicity and race, and yet, men of color are consistently left out of this conversation. Therefore this book is extremely important to serve as a resource for the men of color who are ready to break traditional masculine roles and learn how to become genuinely happy with their lives.

I want to share an introduction from my previous book - A New Conversation With Men. The introduction really summarizes how most of us as men feel yet we seldom speak openly about it. So take a moment to read it and really contemplate its message.

It is my fervent belief that men are frustrated, tired and hungry. They are frustrated because they are trapped in an old paradigm that no longer works. They are frustrated because they are searching for new and better ways to exist as a man yet they have failed in this search. They don't know where to turn, and they are becoming desperate for a new way of being and relating as a man.

They are tired of watching their families fall apart, their health deteriorates, and their wallets are emptied by divorce, materialism, and senseless addictions that rob them of not only their money but their self-esteem and dignity as well. They are tired of working at jobs that they hate just to try to keep up with the Joneses. They are tired of the emptiness and feeling of meaninglessness in their soul that tells them that there has to be another way to exist, yet they don't know how to change.

They are hungry for something new and different, and I believe that something different is A New Conversation with Men.

I know this because I used to be one of those men. I know what it's like to be frustrated, tired, and hungry, and for the last twenty years, I have been removing this frustration, eliminating my exhaustion, and satisfying my hunger to become a better man. As a result, I will admit that my life is now working, and I feel happy and blessed to be a man. I wanted to share my story in hopes of empowering you to follow in my footsteps. I simply want you to become a better man.

This book is written to assist any man who wants to do just that: become a better man. It is written for the man who is sick and tired of being sick and tired, and it is written for that courageous man who refuses to settle for mediocrity and wants to live a life of excellence.

It's been said that, "There is no power in the universe that can stop an idea whose time has come." I believe the time has come for A New Conversation with Men, and there is nothing that can stop it. This book is written to start a new revolution for the hearts, minds and souls of men everywhere, and my hope is that this revolution changes the world for the better.

Can you relate? Do you know what it feels like to be tired, frustrated and hungry? I sure do. And as I mentioned, I was able to remove my frustration, eliminate my exhaustion and satisfy my hunger to become a better man.

Are you ready to do the same?

I believe the answer is yes and this is the reason you've chosen to read this book. There is a part of you that knows your life could be better and it is that part of you that has brought you to this book.

So let's begin by digging into the word masculinity. According to Wikipedia masculinity can be defined as "a set of attributes, behaviors, and roles associated with boys and men." I believe this is an inaccurate definition of masculinity. The word is too subjective to have an objective meaning and I believe this causes a lot of confusion. For example, I believe women can exhibit masculine traits and men can exhibit feminine traits. So the Wikipedia definition can't be accurate.

Rather than try to define it I'd like to share a different way to look at what masculinity actually is. Remember the quote from an earlier chapter; *"You are more than your thoughts, your body, or your feelings. You are a swirling vortex of limitless potential who is here to shake things up and create something new that the Universe has never seen."* If you will accept this as the truth, it will make my explanation a lot easier to understand.

Nikola Tesla was a Serbian-American inventor, electrical engineer, mechanical engineer, and futurist who is best known for his contributions to the design of the modern alternating current (AC) electricity supply. One of his most famous quotes is "If you want to understand the Universe you must think in terms of energy, frequency and vibration." Based on this quote think of masculinity as energy. It is the energy of doing. When we are working on accomplishing things we are using this "doing" energy. For example, if a woman is ambitious and driven to succeed she is using her masculine energy. It has nothing to do with gender. It is an internal feeling that drives her to success.

Therefore, femininity is the energy of being. It is the energy of feeling. When a man is being loving, caring and compassionate he is expressing his feminine energy. Once again it has nothing to do with gender. So it's important to not assign masculinity only to men and femininity only to women. They are simply energies that transcend gender roles.

Recently, there has been a lot of talk about "toxic masculinity". I will assert there is really no such thing. Masculinity isn't toxic although there are definitely men who exhibit toxic behavior. A person who isn't truly in touch with their authentic masculinity drives toxic behavior.

Masculinity is complex and difficult to define but by thinking about it in terms of energy it gives us a framework to build upon.

Since masculinity is based on energy it thereby transcends ethnicity and race. There is no black masculinity or white masculinity there is only the energy of masculinity.

With that being said it's important to understand how the CWBS has had a negative impact on black men and their views about themselves.

Try and imagine what it may have felt like to be sold into slavery and then forced to move to a foreign land. Once there, imagine what it must have been like to be completely stripped of your dignity and humanity and to be seen as property, which was bought and sold to the highest bidder. Can you even imagine how painful it must have been to be chained, whipped and beaten simply because of the color of your skin? What impact did these events have on the black male psyche? And what about being forcibly separated from your family and children? Would this impact how black men viewed being a husband and a father? Thinking about these events, how do you think black men felt about themselves?

And let us not forget about lynchings. Don't you think this violent act had a detrimental effect on black men's self-esteem and how they saw themselves as men? Of course, it did. Even today with police shootings and high incarceration rates, black men have to deal with a multiplicity of psychological and emotional challenges that men of other races don't even have to think about.

Some people would argue this is all in the past and we should be over it by now. In some ways, I agree with that sentiment but it's important to understand how the residual effects of the past in some cases are collectively still impacting black men's lives today.

Therefore I believe it is important to understand how the CWBS has had a detrimental impact on the psyches of black men. At the same time, we must not play the role of victim. We must each take individual responsibility for our own lives and understand we are each individually responsible for our lives turning out the way we want it to. We can no longer blame society for the sins of the past and we simply must commit to creating a better future.

As mentioned, I believe the greatest challenge we have in our world is to redefine what it means to be a man. The roles of manhood and masculinity are changing rapidly for the better and yet most men are rejecting these changing roles. It isn't easy getting men to change their minds after 100's of years of male conditioning but I fervently believe more and more men are beginning to understand that the old ways of being men no longer serve us. It's time to introduce some new ways of being and relating as men and I believe these new ways will improve the quality of men's lives.

As a result of the research and studying I've done over the past twenty years I have concluded, there are five illusions that men hold onto that cause the overwhelming majority of pain and suffering in their lives. These illusions are perpetuated through our families, our cultures and our media. In order to break free from these illusions a man must first become aware that they even exist.

So I would like to share these five illusions with you now.

1. To be a man you must be non-emotional and disconnected.
2. To be a man you must use sexual conquest as a gauge for manhood.
3. To be a man you must have money and material possessions.
4. To be a man you must have titles, positions, and power.
5. To be a man you must constantly compete with and outdo other men.

These five illusions are the foundation of all pain and misery in a man's life. If you will take a moment and really examine them I believe you will see what I mean. To give you a better understanding of how these illusions affect your life I will now break them down and explain each one individually.

1. To be a man you must be non-emotional and disconnected.

I believe that this is the greatest illusion. All other illusions are actually built on top of this one. In our society males are conditioned from a very young age to not feel. We are given the messages that to feel and express those feelings is somehow weak, or worse, feminine. Therefore we start accepting this illusion even as little boys. Think about the powerful messages you received as a young boy, things like, "Big boys don't cry," "Stop being a baby," and "Don't act like a sissy" are the beginning of the acceptance of this illusion. What actually occurs is that we begin to shut down our emotions, and the only way to cope is to express through our intellect. We stop expressing how we feel, and we begin expressing what we think. Of course, there is absolutely nothing wrong with thinking. Using our intellect is an integral and necessary aspect of our humanity, but without our emotions, we become empty, hollow automatons that miss out on the most important aspect of our lives.

This illusion is powerful because as men we accept that the only appropriate feelings we should express are the negative ones. It's absolutely acceptable for a man to express anger and rage in our society without being accused of being less than a man, but if a man expresses joy, sadness, or fear then his masculinity will always be questioned. A good example of this is a television interview that appeared several years ago with Terrell Owens, who was a wide receiver for the Dallas Cowboys football team. After the Cowboys suffered an emotional loss to the New York Giants, Terrell was defending his friend and quarterback Tony Romo. In the interview, Terrell began to cry as he shared openly about how unfair the media was being to his friend. It was obvious that he was deeply saddened by the loss, but he was also saying just how much he cared for his friend. As a result of this interview his masculinity was immediately challenged. The media went into a frenzy about Terrell's emotional interview. Some of the sportscasters accused him of being weak and overly sensitive while others even questioned his sexuality by implying that he might be gay.

The question I pose to you is why is it so unacceptable in our society

Lesson Four: Masculinity

for a man to be emotional? Does it really make us less than men if we are comfortable expressing our feelings and wear our hearts on our sleeves? Who decided that women could be emotional but not men?

This is accepted in our society because we are trapped in the illusion that men are supposed to be non-emotional and disconnected. It is an illusion that has been passed down for generations and the time has come for us to wake up from this illusion. When a man is trapped in this illusion he loses his ability to truly experience life the way it was meant to be. Without his emotions, he will miss out on the most important aspects of his life. His joy, passion, creativity, intuition, connection with his spouse, children, even his faith are all connected to his ability to feel, so it is important that we break free from this illusion and create a new paradigm in which men are comfortable expressing their emotions openly and honestly without fear of having our masculinity challenged.

2. To be a man you must use sexual conquest as a gauge for manhood.

If you get nothing else from this book my hope is that you will get this. This is one of the most destructive illusions perpetuated throughout our society. This illusion contributes to teenage pregnancy, divorce, rape, sexually transmitted diseases, and all sorts of violence. I cannot pinpoint when this illusion began, but I would assume that it has been around since the beginning of time. It really doesn't matter when it started; the question we must ask ourselves is how can we end it?

Think back to your youth and see if you remember how prevalent this illusion was, especially during your younger days. Do you remember when you were young and the only thing you thought about was sex? As a teenager, our minds and our hormones were obsessed with the prospect of having sex. If we are really honest with ourselves we will recognize that almost everything we did in some way led to us trying to attract the opposite sex so that we could engage in the act of sex. We bought our cars to try to attract girls. We played sports hoping that it would attract girls. We bought clothes and kept our hair perfect in hopes of attracting girls. We made money to impress and attract girls. So why were we so obsessed with girls? Because we wanted to have sex! We all believed that by having sex we would validate our manhood, and our friends would cheer for us, and we would be happy and fulfilled. So if we weren't having sex, we usually lied about it just to make sure that we maintained the illusion that we were real men. If we weren't having sex and maintaining this illusion, then we usually felt inadequate and somehow inferior as young men.

Now I would like you to fast forward to the present. If you will take a moment and ask yourself the same questions you will see that most of us as men are still trapped in the same illusion. We buy cars to attract women. We play sports to attract women. We buy clothes and keep our hair perfect to attract women. We make money and spend money to attract and impress women. So why are we so obsessed with attracting women? Because we want to have sex with women!

And when we aren't having sex with women we're usually lying about it to our friends. Can you see the insanity in this? Sexual conquest does not make you a man. It is only an illusion and a temporary fix to your unhappiness. If you are using sex as a gauge for manhood you are trapped in a vicious cycle of addiction and denial and it's time to wake up from the illusion...

3. To be a man you must have money and material possessions.

This illusion is the reason men spend billions upon billions of dollars buying "stuff." Too many of us believe that if we just buy the right house, the right car, the right watch, or the right clothes then we will be viewed as men, and we will gain approval from our friends. This is the reason many of us feel empty and discontented, because we have bought into the illusion that if we accumulate enough "stuff" we will feel fulfilled. Nothing could be further from the truth. This illusion is why so many of us try to "Keep up with the Joneses."

As I think about this illusion, I'm reminded of my high school days when I purchased my first car. My first car was a 1969 Ford Mustang that I absolutely loved. But it wasn't the freedom that came from owning my own car that excited me: it was the fact that in my mind I had now become a man. Of course, I was only seventeen at the time and still living at home, but in my mind I had graduated from adolescence and moved into manhood. (This just goes to show you how this particular illusion really kicks in around our formative high school years.)

Another way that I bought into this illusion was by pretending that I had lots of money even when I didn't. I remember keeping a big wad of cash in my pocket at all times, and I would always have a twenty or a fifty dollar bill on top with lots of one dollar bills on the bottom. Whenever I would be out with my friends I would pull out my wad of cash and pretend that I had a lot more money than I actually did. Since most of my friends didn't have jobs or money I was always seen as "The Man" to my peers. This was definitely a big boost for my ego but it caused me to fall deeper and deeper into the illusion.

These are just two examples of the things some of us as men do when we are trapped in this illusion. Sadly, there are currently lots of men out there today who are still doing the things that I did in high school. (Are you one of them?) They are the ones who have become trapped in the illusion that they must have money and material things to be a man, and I can assure you that they are paying a significant price in terms of their emotional, psychological and spiritual well being.

4. To be a man you must have status, positions and power.

Have you ever noticed how our society adores celebrities, sports figures, and executives? We are taught that, "He who has the gold makes the rules," which implies that the more money you have the "better" you are as a person. The implication is that somehow men who are wealthier or who have higher societal status are somehow "superior" to other men. This is definitely an illusion. The truth of the matter is that monetary wealth does not make you a better man. It may in some ways make your life easier, but it definitely does not make a man superior to other men. The sad part of it is that too many men accept this illusion, and they spend all of their energy trying to move up the societal ladder to validate themselves. They invest all of their time and energy in trying to gain titles and labels, while in reality, they feel empty and unfulfilled. The way that they try to compensate for this emptiness is by acting "superior" even though they really aren't.

I must admit that I was definitely caught in this illusion twenty years ago. Although I did not consider myself to be superior to any other man, I did believe that attaining the title of "Manager" would somehow validate me as a man. Although I did not recognize it at the time, my ambition and drive were actually fueled by my own insecurities about being a man. In my mind, climbing the corporate ladder and becoming successful was a way to prove to myself that I was competent and intelligent. Unfortunately, even after I made it to the top I still felt the same insecurities. Even though I put up the façade of being in control and in charge there was a part of me that was a frightened little boy simply trying to find his way home.

Too many men are currently caught in this illusion of manhood. You can recognize them by their big egos and their arrogance. They parade around town flashing their titles at you and trying to get the external validation they so desperately need. On the outside, they may appear to have it all together, but on the inside they are wounded little boys doing the best they can to maintain their charade.

5. To be a man you must win at all costs and compete against other men.

This is probably the least recognized of all the illusions. Although we seldom talk openly about this, there is an unspoken male law that says that we are supposed to always compete against each other. This can be witnessed on a large scale by corporate corruption. When a man's ego gets inflated he will do any and everything to "stay on top." All rational thinking will go out the window if a man thinks that his competitor is getting ahead of him. Our business schools would teach you that being competitive is the foundation of success, but they will not teach you about the consequences of this overly competitive, macho position that too many men fall victim to.

A perfect example of this on a small scale is an experience I had as a salesman in a hardware store. One day I sold a customer a very expensive bar-b-que grill. The customer wanted to make sure that it had all of the latest technology, and he wanted it to be the "best." I worked with him for a couple of days until I finally put together the grill of his dreams. As he walked out of the store his final comment to me was, "Thanks for helping me put together such an awesome grill. My neighbor is going to be green with envy."

A couple of days later a gentleman shows up and asks to speak to me about purchasing a grill. He specifically asked for me because his neighbor told him that I was very helpful. He raved about how awesome his neighbor's grill was and he said he wanted to purchase one just like it. But then he added that he wanted to make sure that it had at least one feature that his neighbors grill did not have. He did not care what the feature was; as a matter of fact, he even mentioned that he probably wouldn't use the new feature, he simply wanted to make sure that it was better than his neighbor's grill.

This is what happens when you get caught in this illusion. You will do irrational things and then rationalize them by saying you work hard for your money, and you deserve to have the best. Of course, there is nothing wrong with wanting the best for yourself, but when you get trapped in this illusion you will ultimately experience emptiness.

These are the five illusions of manhood that are perpetuated throughout our society. It is absolutely imperative that you recognize these illusions and not be trapped by them. The intention of a new conversation with men is to assist you in breaking free from all of these illusions so I would now like to share some concrete things you can do to break free from the illusions.

1. You must be willing to become aware that the illusion exists.

This is always the most difficult and challenging step, and at the same time, it is always the first step. As soon as you become aware that you are trapped in the illusion, you have already begun waking up from it. Take some time and reflect on these illusions and then write down the one that resonates the most for you. By writing down the illusion it will begin to lose its grip on you. Imagine the illusion as internal darkness and your awareness as eternal light. By shining the light onto the darkness the darkness disappears. Your awareness is the light which will remove the darkness. Challenge yourself to become aware of the illusion you may be caught in.

2. You must be willing to be transformed by the renewing of your mind.

This is what I mean by having a new conversation with men. It means becoming aware of old belief systems, thought patterns, and assumptions that are in your mind that may no longer be working for you. By changing your internal dialog (conversation) you lay the foundation for new ways of being a man. Think of your mind as a garden and all of your thoughts as seeds. Whatever seed (thought) you plant has to grow. If you are planting negative seeds guess what grows? If you are planting positive seeds what do you think will sprout up? Transforming your mind means that you make a conscious effort in recognizing what types of seeds you are planting. The more conscious you become the more likely you are to plant positive seeds.

This also means that you become conscious of all of the things that you are allowing to be planted in your mind. This means that you should limit your exposure to all of the negative seeds that are planted by our media. So do yourself a favor and disconnect from too much television.

3. You must be willing to heal and reconnect to your emotions.

This is definitely our greatest challenge as men. As I mentioned, we are conditioned not to feel, but it is our responsibility to go against the societal conditioning and become courageous enough to begin our emotional-healing process. Until you learn to heal and feel there will always be something missing in your life.

4. You must seek support.

You must understand that you cannot do this alone. I understand how difficult it is for men to seek support, but the fact remains you must seek help. I don't care if you go to therapy, join a men's group, join AA, or go to a church group. It is important that you surround yourself with like-minded men who can support and challenge you to become the best man you can be. Gaining the courage to seek support is a surefire way to help you break free from any of these illusions. I highly recommend that you join our online community at www.anewconversationwithmen.com, because it is filled with resources designed to help you break free from these illusions, and it will put you in contact with other men who are on the same journey as you. They can serve as role models and mentors for you and help you recognize that you are never alone.

5. You must develop a spiritual connection that works for you.

This does not necessarily mean that you have to join a church or other religious organization. It means that you must come to your own understanding that there is a power greater than yourself in the universe. By connecting to this power it will give you strength, faith, and courage to break free from the illusions and live a more rewarding and fulfilling life. Once you develop this connection it is your responsibility to nurture it and ensure that you stay connected to it.

So there you have them, the five illusions of manhood:

1. *To be a man you must be non-emotional and disconnected.*
2. *To be a man you must use sexual conquest as a gauge for manhood.*
3. *To be a man you must have money and material possessions.*
4. *To be a man you must have status, positions and power.*
5. *To be a man you must win at all costs and compete against other men.*

And these are the five things you can do to wake up from the illusions:

1. *You must be willing to become aware that the illusion exists.*
2. *You must be willing to be transformed by the renewing of your mind.*
3. *You must be willing to heal and reconnect to your emotions.*
4. *You must seek support.*
5. *You must develop a spiritual connection that works for you.*

In order to make the world a better place we must recognize these illusions and remove them from our collective psyches. It begins with each man waking up and choosing to break free from these illusions. In doing so, the world will be a much better place for everyone.

Are you willing to look at the man in the mirror and ask him to change his ways? If the answer is yes I want to share another powerful lesson I've learned about men and masculinity.

Back in the late 80's or early 90's I attended a lecture by a man named Marvin Allen. He was a nationally known therapist who was recognized for his work dealing with men and the changing roles of masculinity.

The lecture was titled "The Five Masks of Masculinity" and in the lecture, Mr. Allen talked about how men begin wearing psychological masks as a way to deal with their repressed emotions. His theory was that when we, as children, experience any type of physical and emotional trauma, our minds try to compensate by creating defense mechanisms to minimize the pain. As we begin to shut down our emotions, we begin to rely strictly on our intellects. In order to cope, we create these metaphoric masks, which then become our pseudo-identity. In other

Lesson Four: Masculinity

words, it isn't who we really are; it's our ego developing an alter ego. This alter ego then becomes our identity, and we begin playing out the roles from behind the masks.

The reason I remember this lesson so vividly is because at the time of the lesson, I was still wearing my metaphorical mask. I was trapped behind this mask and pretending to be someone that I wasn't, and as I listened to the lecture, I realized that I had to do whatever it took to remove my mask and become authentic. As a result of that lecture, I recommitted myself to discovering who I really was, and that was one of the things that propelled me to continue my journey of self-discovery and remove my mask of self-deception.

So now I would like to share the five masks with you. As you read these, simply recognize that there is a small part of you that may be found in each of the masks. Try not to judge them as good or bad, right or wrong. Simply see them as artificial identities that you may have developed to protect yourself. The good news is, as soon as you become aware that you are wearing one, it begins to loosen its grip on you, and before you know it, you won't even be wearing it at all. But the key is to acknowledge that you may be wearing one so that you can then break through your denials.

As you read these, try to recognize which one resonates with you. I can assure you that if you are truly honest with yourself you will immediately recognize which one you may or may not be wearing. Just try to stay focused so that you connect with the one that is most appropriate for you. (The titles that Mr. Allen used were slightly different from the ones I am using here. I have modified them just a little for my own understanding and explanation.)

Here are the five masks:

Mr. Nice Guy

Mr. Tough as Nails

Mr. Money Bags

Mr. Gigolo

Mr. Stuck in His Head

I would now like to give my interpretations and explanations of what these masks represent and how they can unconsciously affect our lives. It is important that you really take the time to recognize which one "fits" for you and then take the time to recognize and ultimately remove the mask. Just remember that this can be extremely challenging and confusing at first. But if you will take some time and contemplate the lessons in this chapter it can serve as a springboard for your awakening and transformation. Remember, the first step in removing your mask is to simply become aware of which one you are wearing. By becoming aware, you open the door to transforming your life for the better, but you must be willing to walk through the door so that the masks are no longer necessary.

Mr. Nice Guy

As I listened to the facilitator speak about the Mr. Nice Guy mask I was absolutely captivated by his presentation. Everything he said seemed to hit home for me, and I immediately recognized that this was the mask that I had been hiding behind all of my life.

As I reflected back over my life, I could see how wearing this mask had done two things. The first thing it had done was keep me from feeling and expressing my own real emotions. As a result of some physical and emotional trauma in my childhood, I had learned to repress and shut down how I really felt. For example, instead of being able to express my anger, I would usually smile and pretend that I really wasn't mad. No matter how angry I felt inside I would hold it in and pretend that the anger wasn't there. Before I knew it I had completely lost my ability to feel and express anger. This had always been a real problem for me, yet I never recognized it until this lecture. As I thought about it deeply, I could see how hiding behind this mask had had a very negative impact on my self-esteem and sense of self worth. Because I was always denying my true feelings I was constantly negating myself and putting other people's needs ahead of my own, which led to the second thing that wearing the mask had done to me.

The second thing it had done was cause me to become an incessant people pleaser. Since I had such a difficult time expressing my true feelings it was impossible for me to really feel good about myself. To try to compensate for my feelings of inadequacy I developed an insatiable need to please other people. This need to please became my Mr. Nice Guy mask, which I wore to not only get people to like me, but also to try to get them to love me. The sad part is that as long as I was wearing that mask I could never experience their love. I had to be willing to remove my mask so that I could be myself and allow people to love me for me and not for the fake Mr. Nice Guy mask I was wearing.

These were just two of the things I learned during this lecture, and as a result, I spent the next ten years learning how to remove my mask and become comfortable with who I really am. It wasn't easy, but I can assure you that removing my mask was probably the greatest gift that I have ever given myself.

As you're thinking about these masks, I must also inform you of the good news. The good news is that there is always a flip side to wearing a mask. As you become aware of your mask and begin to remove it, you will also begin to recognize that wearing the mask also brought you a gift. You may not be able to recognize the gifts at first, but I can assure you that they are there waiting to be discovered.

Here are just a few of the gifts I received as a result of wearing my Mr. Nice Guy mask:

Wearing my mask actually helped me become a more caring and compassionate person.

Wearing my mask challenged me to become a positive, optimistic person.

Wearing my mask challenged me to question things more deeply and become a lifelong student of learning.

Each person's experience will obviously be different, but as soon as you become willing to recognize that you have a mask on you actually begin taking it off. So to assist you in this process I'd like to ask you a couple of questions if you think you may be wearing the Mr. Nice Guy mask:

Do you have difficulty expressing the emotion of anger? Are you constantly seeking other peoples approval? Do you always pretend that everything is all right even when it's not? Do you have difficulty accepting compliments? Do you feel "stuck" in life?

Take a moment and ponder these questions. If you answered yes to any of them then it's quite possible that you are trapped behind the Mr. Nice Guy mask. Spend a little time reflecting over your life and see if this mask resonates with you.

Let's move on to the next mask.

Mr. Tough as Nails

Have you ever met a man who seldom smiles and appears angry most of the time? Do you know of anyone who never shows any emotion except anger and negativity and flies into a rage over some of the most insignificant situations? Do you know anyone who never has a kind word to say about anything or anybody? Do you know of anyone who is always ready, willing, and able to start a fight for the smallest provocation?

If you do, then there is a very good chance that you know someone who is wearing the Mr. Tough as Nails mask. In a society that teaches men that they must be tough in order to be a man, it's no wonder so many men embrace this mask. This mask goes hand in hand with the first illusion of manhood which I discussed earlier in this chapter. The first illusion was, *"To be a man you must be non-emotional and disconnected."*

When a man wears this mask he loses his ability to experience positive emotions. As a matter of fact, he will do everything in his power never to show emotion. The only emotion he is comfortable with is anger or rage, and therefore it is usually the only emotion he will express. The sad part is that he usually has a heart of gold beneath his rage, yet he does not know how to connect to it. His defense mechanism of anger sometimes covers up his deep feelings of sadness and fear, so he uses his anger to feel a false sense of power and control. Mr. Tough as Nails can be controlling and manipulative, and he will deny his true feelings by creating a wall of anger and non- attachment. If you feel that this is the mask you may be wearing ask yourself these questions: Do you get angry easily? Do you have difficulty smiling and feeling happy? Do you rationalize your anger by saying that is just the way men are? Do you notice that your body is usually tense and constricted? Do you judge men who can verbally express their emotions as being weak, soft or sissies?

Remember the key to removing your mask is to simply become aware that you have one. Simply take some time to see if you recognize yourself wearing either of these masks. It is extremely important that you pay attention to your body as you're reading this. Try and notice any physical discomfort inside of you. If reading this triggers anything inside of you then that means that you are definitely on the right track to identifying with the mask you may be wearing. Try to recognize the feeling within and just let it move through you.

Mr. Money Bags

This mask is a direct result of the third illusion of manhood, which is, *To be a man you must have money and material possessions.* You will recognize Mr. Money Bags by his attachment to material things. He is the guy that is always trying to impress you with his "stuff." It could be his car or clothes or jewelry, or maybe his bank account. No matter which one it is he is always making sure that you see his "stuff." This is the same guy who will try to impress a woman by spending an insane amount of money on a first date with a woman who he doesn't even know yet. This is really his way of saying, "I know you won't like me for who I am, so instead, I will try to 'buy' your love for me." What he doesn't realize is that his need to impress people is driven by his mask. And as long as he wears the mask, no amount of money will ever fill the emptiness he feels inside. If you feel connected to this mask ask yourself these questions:

Do you brag about your "stuff" to others? Are you always trying to keep up with the Joneses? Are you constantly lending money to friends that never pay you back? Are your credit cards maxed out because of excessive spending? Do you spend unnecessary amounts of money on things to try to impress others? Do you relate to this mask? Let it sink in as we move on to the next one.

Mr. Gigolo

Remember illusion number two? *To be a man you must use sexual conquest as a gauge for manhood.* This is the foundation of Mr. Gigolo's behavior. Mr. Gigolo is so caught up in this illusion that he always justifies his actions by asserting what a "man" he is whenever he has sex. This is one of the reasons why some men brag about impregnating women without having any intention of being a father. Getting a woman pregnant is a way of a man's saying that he has sexual power, and it temporarily inflates his already deflated ego.

A man who is trapped behind this mask will constantly seek validation by having sex with as many women as possible. Unfortunately, his behavior is driven by a deep sense of inadequacy, and no matter how many women he sleeps with, his insecurities still remain. Each conquest gives him a temporary high that is short lived because it is based only on the physical aspect of sex. What he does not realize is what he really craves is emotional intimacy and connection; unfortunately, his mask will not allow him to have that which he so desperately craves. All sexual addictions are driven by this mask. If this mask is not removed it becomes impossible for a man to create loving, connected, monogamous relationships. No matter how much a woman may love a man, and no matter what she may do to satisfy him sexually, if a man is trapped behind this mask he will constantly seek sexual conquest in many different forms. These include but are not limited to pornography, infidelity, and even child molestation.

In our sex-crazed culture, this mask is becoming more and more widespread, and men are beginning to exhibit this negative behavior at earlier ages than ever. If you feel you may be trapped behind this particular mask ask yourself these questions:

Do you feel a "letdown" after sex? Do you find yourself addicted to pornography? Do you spend time in strip clubs without telling your spouse? Are you obsessed with sex and are never truly satisfied with it? Do you demand sex from your spouse even when she says no?

It takes an incredible amount of courage to answer these questions honestly. I hope you take the time to contemplate these questions and see if you identify with this particular mask. If so, just remember that the simple recognition of the mask begins the process of removing it.

Our final mask is:

Mr. Stuck in His Head

I once had a personal coaching session with a very beautiful woman who complained about her husband's lack of emotional availability. Her complaint was that he did not show affection, and he was obsessively controlling. She said that he happened to be an engineer and that it was important to him to analyze everything that she did. He had a PhD, and he made sure that everyone knew it especially her.

As she sat there crying, she shared how he was extremely anal about everything and always wanted to "intellectualize" her actions. He would quote case studies and technical journals about why men and women behaved the way they did and he always spoke to her as though he was her professor instead of her mate. He was very good at reciting statistics and theories, but he could not speak openly about his feelings or share how he actually felt about her.

After a year or so of counseling (with a therapist) they divorced. I coached her for approximately six months after her divorce and she eventually moved on with her life to another city.

A year or so later I was giving a talk at the men's council and I was speaking on why it's so difficult for men to express their feelings. I talked about the importance of getting out of our heads and into our hearts and I shared some of my personal struggles with this issue. I talked about the phenomenon of being "stuck in the head," and it really got a lot of men's attention. Apparently, there were a lot of men who had experienced this, and they were definitely relating to my talk.

After my talk, a man walked up to me and told me just how much he enjoyed it. He said that he really related to my story because he had always had difficulty expressing his feelings. He said he wished he would have heard the talk a few years earlier because he's being "stuck in his head" had caused him to lose his marriage. He said that maybe if he had heard the talk back then he would not have lost the woman that he truly loved and cared about. After a few moments of conversing we eventually started to talk about his ex-wife, and it turned out that she was the woman that I had been coaching a couple of years earlier.

I never told him about my sessions with his ex-wife, but I did tell him that it was possible for him to create a new love affair as long as he was willing to get out of his head and into his heart. He definitely agreed and told me that he was committed to doing just that.

Mr. Stuck in His Head is probably the least recognizable of all the masks. Most of us as men probably analyze things too much, but that does not mean that we are wearing this particular mask. If you think you may be wearing this mask ask yourself these questions:

Are you able to express how you feel versus what you think? Can you make the distinction between the two? Has anyone ever told you that you think too much in relationships? Are you an accountant, engineer, or mathematician who gets lost in numbers and statistics? Do you have difficulty having fun and laughing out loud?

Spend some time with these questions and see if they resonate with you. If you feel that you are stuck in your head it's important that you get out of your head and into your heart if you ever want to feel fully alive.

So there you have them, the Five Masks of Masculinity: Mr. Nice Guy, Mr. Tough as Nails, Mr. Money Bags, Mr. Gigolo and Mr. Stuck in His Head

Did you relate to any of them? Do you already know which is your strong suit? If you recognize which is the one you are wearing, are you willing to take it off? Are you willing to do whatever it takes to remove the mask and become the authentic male that you were destined to be?

If the answer is yes then the first thing you must do is embrace *A New Conversation with Men*. This simply means that you become willing to see yourself from a different point of view. This new conversation will

Lesson Four: Masculinity

allow you to become open-minded to change, which opens the door to your transformation. The next thing you must be willing to do is to heal your heart. This is the key that unlocks the door to removing your masks. It is probably the most important and at the same time most difficult thing you must do.

But rest assured you have everything you need already inside of yourself to change. It may be a good idea to reread the chapter on "The Cure". It provided you with some specific steps you can take to move through any emotional or psychological challenge you may be dealing with. The only thing that's missing is your willingness to change.

Make a commitment to yourself to change and in doing so you will have joined a new conversation with men and assisted in creating a new paradigm of masculinity that will help heal the world.

"When the power of love overcomes the love of power the world will know peace."

Jimi Hendrix

LESSON FIVE:
Love

I was flipping through the channels on my Sling TV app and I ran across a show on the Oprah Winfrey Network called Black Love. I was intrigued by the title and decided to check it out. I knew nothing about the show but I must admit that I was pleasantly surprised about the content. The show featured black couples talking openly and honestly about the challenges of relationships and marriage. It was refreshing to see and hear the conversations and it showed a different side of black relationships that you seldom see in mainstream media.

The creator of the show Tommy Oliver put it this way when he was asked about the inspiration behind the show:

"Part of it was so much of what we see on reality and scripted TV is an incredibly poor rendering of black families and black married families in particular. For us, we knew that there were information and images that we wanted to see, and we assumed that many other people wanted to see it as well. Most TV is generated by ratings and advertising, so drama and sensationalism tend to do well. Beyond that, it comes down to the people who are creating the content and have the ability to greenlight content. When you are not a part of the decision-making process, you don't have the ability to really inform what you see and shape the narrative, and a lot of that is why we end up with these poor renderings [of black marriages] that are dangerous to the psyche of folks who want to get married, or want to see themselves and the aspirational elements of what they are endeavoring toward."

I truly enjoyed the episode and I believe it is a much-needed show for people of all ethnicities to see because it definitely goes against the CWBS's portrayal of black people and marriage/relationships. We are constantly bombarded with images of single mothers and deadbeat dads so it was definitely refreshing to see the love, connection, intimacy and openness of the couples on the show.

Although I truly enjoyed the show and there is definitely a need for this type of show showcasing people of color creating and maintaining healthy marriages/relationships, I think it's important to understand there is really no such thing as "black love".

Let me explain what I mean.

When it comes to showcasing people of color the CWBS primarily focuses on negative stereotypes about us. As mentioned, we see rappers objectifying women, athletes hanging out in strip clubs making it rain by throwing money at strippers and incidences of domestic violence and abuse. Seldom do you see black men and women in loving, nurturing sensitive and caring interactions with each other?

Therefore, the CWBS would have you believe there is a "white" way of relating and behaving and a "black" way of relating and behaving. Of course, collectively speaking, the "white" way is seen as the "good" way and the "black" way is seen as the "bad" way.

The truth is there is no "white" way or "black" way. There is only the right way of relating and behaving. Being loving, nurturing, sensitive and caring has nothing to do with a person's ethnicity. It has everything to do with their ontological (the branch of metaphysics dealing with the nature of being) makeup. So using the term Black Love implies we as people of color somehow love differently and that is not the case. Unfortunately, too many of us as people of color buy into the stereotypes of mainstream media and therefore believe our love is somehow different. It is not. Love is love and it isn't bound by skin color.

I have absolutely no problem with naming the show Black Love and I think in the context in which it is used the title is perfect. However, I think it's important to understand that love has no color and relationships are built upon an emotional framework. Without the emotional framework, relationships are destined to fail because in order to be relational we must be willing to be emotional and being emotional has nothing to do with race.

Lesson Five: Love

With that being said, why is it so difficult for us to create great relationships?

As a man who has been happily married for the past 17 years, I would like to share some of the lessons I've learned which have allowed me to create a partnership that works and a marriage that is rewarding and fulfilling.

First I'd like to share the mistakes I made in my first marriage, which obviously ended in divorce.

The first time I got married I was 21 years old. Although I didn't realize this at the time, I got married for all the wrong reasons. As I look back in retrospect I realize I was on a societal rollercoaster doing everything I thought a man was supposed to do to be happy. In my mind, I believed being married would help me climb the corporate ladder of success and by having a family, I would prove that I was a responsible and mature man and that would help advance my career.

The fact is, I was too young and emotionally insecure to be getting married, and as mentioned, I was doing it for all the wrong reasons. The sad part is there was a part of me that knew I wasn't ready to be married but I was too afraid to listen to my heart and I rationalized in my head that I could fix whatever might be wrong in my relationship. I remember standing in front of the minister during the wedding ceremony and my heart was screaming "don't do it!" while my mind kept saying "you can fix it." I didn't trust my heart and ultimately it proved to be right.

To be honest I really didn't have a bad marriage. We really didn't fight that often or have a lot of drama. But something was missing that I really couldn't explain. I have now come to know the thing that was missing was intimacy and connection. I had absolutely no idea what these things were while I was married but I now know they are the keys to creating great relationships.

Intimacy is our ability to In-To-Me- See our deepest thoughts feelings and beliefs about ourselves. When we can be open and honest with our partners about how we really feel and what we really think and believe we create intimacy. Once we create intimacy we then create the connection. The connection is what our hearts long for but unfortunately most of us do not have the emotional intelligence to create authentic intimacy and connection.

I'm reminded of a quote by Barbara De Angelis: *The more connections you and your lover make, not just between your bodies, but between your minds, your hearts, and your souls, the more you will strengthen the fabric of your relationship, and the more real moments you will experience together."*

This is the reason intimacy and connection are so important. When we are able to create "real" moments we create intimacy and when are able to create intimacy we create connections.

As mentioned in the chapter on masculinity most of us as men are conditioned to believe that men are not supposed to feel. We are conditioned to believe that women are more emotional than men and men aren't supposed to be in touch with their emotions. Herein lies the problem for most men. If we are disconnected from our emotions we cannot create intimacy and connection. This is why it is so important to do your emotional healing work so you can connect on an emotional level.

You must understand the most important relationship you will ever create is the relationship with yourself. This means knowing exactly how you feel, how you think and what you believe.

As I reflect back over my first marriage I can see why I didn't have intimacy and connection. First of all, I had a lot of emotional baggage I was carrying around because of my traumatic childhood. Secondly, I believed if I bought my wife a house, provided for my family and was a good husband then I should have been happy. Unfortunately, it didn't work. I did all of those things and was still not happy. Because of my lack of intimacy and connection I couldn't give my wife what she needed most, which was me. She didn't care about the house or material possessions. She only cared about me. But because of my insecurities and emotional issues I didn't believe that. I simply did not know how to connect with her on an emotional level.

Relationships are a two way street and I definitely took responsibility

Lesson Five: Love

for my part in my failed marriage but I have to admit I wasn't the only one to blame. My wife was also emotionally disconnected so it's no wonder our marriage fell apart. We simply were not able to create authentic intimacy and connection in our marriage and therefore it ended up in divorce.

After my divorce, I had a lot of difficulties in creating healthy relationships. I remember immediately after my divorce declaring I would never get married again. Unconsciously, the pain was too great to risk trying again so I didn't date for over a year. Once I did decide to date again my relationships were disasters.

After a few failed relationships I begin to notice a pattern. My relationships would last 3-4 weeks and they would end with the women telling me they cared too much about me to stay in the relationship. Think about that for a moment. How much sense does that make to you? How can you care about someone and then leave them? I was completely confused.

After some self-reflection and research, I uncovered the problem. One thing that each of the women said was I was emotionally unavailable and therefore there was no reason for them to continue a relationship with me. At first it didn't make sense but upon further investigation I learned exactly what they meant.

Let me explain by sharing one of my relationship experiences with you.

I met a woman at the gym who was absolutely gorgeous. On a scale of 1-10, she was honestly a 12. She had a near perfect body, had a great job, drove a nice car and was extremely fun to be with. After a couple of dates I asked her if she would like to go to a pool party one of my neighbors was having. She agreed and on the day of the party she showed up in a 2-piece bikini and she was absolutely stunning. We walked down the street to my neighbor's house and when we walked in all of my friends jaws literally dropped. Of course I was filled with pride as my friends all stared at how beautiful she was and of course my ego received a big boost. We had a wonderful time at the party and afterwards we went back to my place and had a few drinks and a few laughs. She told me she was happy that my friends found her so attractive and she specifically wore the bikini to impress my friends. I told her thanks for making me look so good and I appreciated her allowing me to show her off to my friends.

A few days later I was hanging out with my friends and of course, the topic of conversation was my date. They all wanted to know where and how we met and the single guys wanted to know the secret to finding such a beautiful woman.

Interestingly enough, no one ever asked what type of woman she was. The only thing they were concerned with was her external physical beauty and of course so was I. What I realize in retrospect is I was definitely proud to have my friends admire me for having been with such a beautiful woman but deep down inside I really felt insecure about my ability to create a deep relationship that would allow me to keep her.

Internally I had a deep fear of abandonment and it would ultimately sabotage my relationship. Having a fear of abandonment caused me to try to do everything right to keep her in a relationship with me. I was extremely nice and supportive, I was very attentive to her needs and I was able to satisfy her sexually. On the surface it appeared I was doing everything right. But unfortunately, my relationship pattern showed up again so I was obviously doing everything wrong.

One night while lying in bed she asked me to share how I really felt about her. She also asked why I never mentioned if I missed her when she was away. As I thought about it, I knew I wasn't in love with her but I also knew I cared deeply about her. But I honestly didn't know what to say. I really enjoyed being with her but I honestly didn't know how to share how I really felt about her. She then made a comment about my inability to express how I felt and she said she was afraid of getting emotionally close to me because she knew I was emotionally unavailable.

I then became angry because I thought I was doing everything right in the relationship and now she was saying I wasn't emotionally available. I tried to explain to her that my actions should have told her how much I cared about her but her reply was my actions couldn't express how I felt about her, only the words from my heart could relay

Lesson Five: Love

the feelings I had for her. Since I couldn't verbalize how I felt she didn't believe that I really cared about her.

After that conversation, our relationship changed and eventually, she left saying she cared too much about me to stay in the relationship. When we broke up she was crying and saying that she had so much love to give to me but she knew I was not capable of reciprocating that love back to her and she wasn't willing to give so much and not receive it back from me. She said that was her reason for leaving and at the time I truly didn't understand her reasoning but because of my growth, I now know exactly what she meant and why she left.

Although I was sad when she left a part of me was in complete denial. I rationalized it in my head by saying she doesn't know what she's missing. I'm a good man and I know there are lots of fish in the sea so I'll just have to find the one that is right for me. I denied my sadness and never admitted to myself that I really didn't want to break up with her. She was an amazing woman but I simply didn't have the emotional tools to create intimacy and connection with her at the time so I rationalized it by saying it was her loss, not mine. Deep down inside though I really wished she hadn't left.

I waited several months before I started dating again and unfortunately I experienced the same result. Women just kept leaving me.

Then I received a miracle. I was having a conversation, actually, it wasn't a conversation, and it was more of a pity party about women with a female friend of mine. I was complaining to her about how women always say they want a good man but when a good man shows up why do they always leave.

My friend looked at me and said something that shook me to my core. "Michael, if one person calls you a jackass you probably shouldn't worry about it. But if two or more do you better get a saddle. Have you not noticed you're the only common denominator in all of your relationships? Maybe the women aren't the problem maybe it's you."

Her words penetrated my psyche and for the first time in my life, I recognized I was the problem. I immediately understood if I wanted to create great relationships I had to be willing to look at myself and take full responsibility for my participation in relationships.

One of the things that challenged me to change was my commitment to wanting to create a rewarding and fulfilling partnership. I didn't necessarily want to get married I simply wanted to know what it felt like to truly love someone. I had friends that had wonderful marriages and I had read several books from couples that were genuinely happy with their relationships so I concluded it was possible for me to create one also. After having that conversation with my friend I became very self-introspective and I started dissecting my patterns in relationships and taking full responsibility for my participation in them.

As mentioned in the earlier chapter, I had to be willing to look at some deep emotional scars I had been carrying around for years. I had to be willing to heal my heart and make peace with my past and move through the emotional trauma I had gone through in my childhood. Nothing sabotages relationships like unhealed trauma. If you're having difficulty with relationships and identify with my story it's possible you have some unhealed trauma you need to confront. Be willing to do your inner work and commit to your own growth and you will lay the foundation for creating a relationship that works.

Of course relationships and marriages can be difficult but I am living proof it is possible to create a love affair that is rewarding, fulfilling and satisfying. Unfortunately, sometimes relationships and marriages will come to an end so I wanted to share an article I wrote titled Bouncing Back From Divorce. It summarizes what I've been saying so far in this chapter and I'm sure it will provide you with some insights that can support you if you're dealing with divorce or a breakup.

"I WANT A DIVORCE!" Although it's been over 30 years since I heard these words, I still remember the shock and uncertainty I felt when my former wife screamed them at me. Although I knew there were problems in our marriage, I really didn't believe that they were insurmountable. I knew that I was unhappy and felt trapped in a situation that I could not get out of, but now that I had a way out, I was unprepared to deal with it. I remember sitting up late that night and pondering what my next step should be. Should I go along with it and end our six-year marriage? What about the kids? Should I fight for custody? What will my friends and co-workers think? Where will I live? Should I give up the house? These were just a few of the questions running through my mind, and I had absolutely no idea how I was going to answer them.

The first few days after her divorce requests were terrible. We would not speak to each other or even make direct eye contact. Although we continued to sleep in the same bed, we were emotionally miles apart from one another. We would simply go through our regular routines and walk past each other without saying a word. I could feel the tension between us, but I felt powerless to do anything. Every time I attempted to speak with her, our conversations would erupt into a shouting match. It appeared that there was nothing that could be done to save our marriage.

After several days, I was able to put my sadness and anger aside to try and make some rational decisions. I decided that it would be best if we at least attempted to save our marriage. There were several factors that prompted my decision. First of all, there were my children. As a child, I remember how much I missed not having a father in my life. I always envied my friends who had fathers, and I remember making a conscious decision to be a good father if I ever had children of my own. My children and I were very close, so I definitely wanted to minimize any pain they would experience. Another reason that I thought it would be best to stay together was financial. I knew that if we were to divorce, it would be extremely difficult for me to make it on my own while paying child support and possibly maintaining two households since my wife was a stay-at-home mom. Last but not least (and I'm not proud of this), I was really afraid of what my friends and employees would think of me. In their eyes, I had a perfect life. I had created this image of having it all together, and the thought of going through with this divorce would shatter that image. That really scared me and filled me with shame and embarrassment.

I convinced my wife to try marriage counseling. I told her that I really wanted to try and work things out, so we should at least give it a try. She agreed, and we began counseling. After several sessions, it became obvious that our marriage was not going to work out. I discovered that I really wanted out of the marriage, but I was too afraid to say it. All the reasons that I tried to make the marriage work were wrong. I never asked myself the two most important questions of my life: 1. Do I really love her? 2. Do I really want to spend the rest of my life with her? As a result of our counseling, I realized that the answer was "No" to both questions.

Once we knew that the divorce was inevitable, I decided to make it as amicable as possible. I sat down with her and said we should try to make this as simple and painless as possible. Fortunately, she agreed, and we were able to decide on how our possessions would be divided up. We were even able to work out visitation with the children. As a matter of fact, our divorce was so amicable that we used the same attorney to handle the divorce (if you are currently going through a divorce, my suggestion is that you do everything in your power to separate on good terms. Although this is extremely difficult, I can assure you that if you put your ego aside and try and work things out together, everybody wins in the end). I must admit that I am truly grateful to my ex-wife for being willing to work things out the way we did. I am forever indebted to her for never speaking badly to our children about me and for making sure that we worked together as parents to help our children handle the whole ordeal. Our willingness to work together to raise our children has paid off with three emotionally and psychologically well-adjusted children that we are both extremely proud of.

After the divorce was final, I found myself in unknown territory. This was actually the first time I had really failed at anything so major and life-changing. I did not know what to expect, but intuitively I knew that I would get through it. At the time, I was somewhat isolated and alone. I really did not have any close friends to talk to, so I simply kept to myself and tried to handle it alone. One of the first declarations I made was to never get married again. Marriage was a difficult and painful experience, and I concluded that I did not want to experience the pain and loss of a divorce ever again. To avoid the potential pain of relationships, I simply immersed myself in my work

After a few months, I decided to break out of my isolation and at least start going out again. Although I wasn't looking for a relationship, I did at least want to have some companionship. The problem I had with going out was that I was still ashamed and embarrassed because of my divorce, and I felt as if I had this huge neon letter 'D' stamped on my forehead. My feelings of inadequacy and failure made it extremely difficult to really connect with anyone, so most of the time I simply would go to clubs and dance a little without having much conversation.

Within approximately six months, I started to long for a relationship. I was tired of being alone, and I really missed having a partner to share life with. I decided to try and date to see what would happen. My first few relationships after my divorce were disasters. Although I did not know this at the time, I was absolutely terrified of intimacy. I had all sorts of trouble connecting on an emotional level with women because I was still scarred emotionally from my divorce. After several failures, I began to recognize a pattern in my relationships. The first thing I noticed was that my relationships never lasted more than 3-4 weeks. Within that time period, something would happen that would terminate the relationship. In most cases, the women were the ones who were saying that they weren't ready for a relationship. If they weren't leaving, I was the one making excuses about why I needed to end the relationship. I had devised some pretty good excuses for ending relationships, like being too busy at work or trying to be a good father to my children, but the truth was that I was terrified of experiencing the pain I had associated with relationships.

After a couple of years, I met a woman that I really enjoyed being with. We had great chemistry and had a lot in common. After dating her for over a year, I began having deep feelings for her and decided that I really wanted to make a commitment to an exclusive relationship with her. When I told her how I felt, her response really caught me by surprise. She told me that she really liked me a lot and would like to develop a committed relationship with me, but she knew that I was emotionally unavailable to her, so she did not want to invest her feelings into a guy that could not reciprocate her love. I felt rejected and angry and did not know how to respond to her comment. As a result, the relationship ended, and there I was, alone again.

The good news is that I really listened to what she had to say. I recognized that I was the problem, not her. I was able to see that I was the reason my relationships weren't working out, and I decided to do something about it. I began my own inner journey to heal my heart so that I would no longer keep pushing women out of my life. I followed M. Scott Peck's advice and took the road less traveled, and I definitely became a better man as a result of it.

After being on my fifteen-year personal journey and learning to love myself, I decided that I really did want to remarry. Since I took the time to understand the how's and the why's of my past relationship failures, I was able to finally create loving and supportive relationships without the fear of intimacy or abandonment. As a result of my commitment to my own personal growth, I was able to create a relationship that really works for me, which ultimately resulted in me getting remarried and creating a marriage that really nurtures and supports me. I really enjoy the emotional security that comes from having a spouse that loves and adores me, and I'm truly grateful that I took the time to understand the importance of having authentic relationships.

Great relationships take effort and commitment, but ultimately they are definitely life's greatest treasure. If you are having difficulty with relationships, been through or are going through a divorce, or have a deep fear of commitment, take the time to heal your heart, and it will open the door to creating great relationships.

Good luck!

So now I would like to share 10 keys to creating healthy relationships. I can assure you that if you apply these keys to your life, you will create rewarding, fulfilling, and intimately connected relationships.

Number 1:

Develop a healthy relationship with yourself. For most men, I can assure you it is very uncomfortable for them to say, "I love myself." Why? Because for some people that may sound a little arrogant, a little cocky, a little narcissistic. The truth is, if you don't love yourself, you cannot love another person. It's not possible because all relationships begin with you. The first thing you have to be willing to do is create a healthy relationship with yourself. When you look in the mirror, ask yourself what do you see? Do you see someone that's trustworthy? Do you see someone that's lovable? Do you see someone that's dependable? Do you see someone in that mirror that you would want to be in a relationship with? Ask yourself that question honestly because that's where relationships begin.

They begin with you. If you want to create healthy relationships, start with yourself. Sometimes that means we have to take a break from relationships with other people and spend some time developing a relationship with ourselves. This may be uncomfortable or seem a little weird, but rest assured, it is the first thing you must do. Too many times, we want to point our fingers at the women in our lives, but the fact remains that if we want to create healthy relationships, it always begins with the man in the mirror. We must take complete responsibility for our relationships and not blame anyone else except ourselves. Once we do this, we lay the foundation for great relationships.

Number 2:

Make relationships top priority. In our culture and in our society, a man's job has basically been three things: procreate, protect and provide. This has been true since the beginning of time. Think about it. What was a caveman's primary responsibility? He was supposed to find a cave to keep his little cavewoman happy and warm, and then he had to go out there to find food and make sure that he kept the dinosaurs from eating his family. Provide and protect.

Unfortunately, too many men are still trying to do that. They believe that if they just do these three things, then they will be happy. What we really need to do if we're going to make relationships top priority is to connect; not just provide and protect, but connect. Connection takes emotions, and too many times men do not have the emotional awareness to connect, which is a major cause of relationship failure.

What we usually do is focus all of our attention on our jobs, our bills, our cars, our staff, and our kids, but we aren't doing anything to connect in our relationships. We aren't doing anything to deepen our connection.

The sad part is that a lot of men will go through life and work at a career, raise their kids, and do everything they can to try and keep up with the Joneses. Then they get close to retirement and start asking themselves, "What am I going to do?"

As soon as they retire and they're at home with their wives on a full-time basis, it's total chaos because now they have to connect with their spouse, but they don't know how to do that.

If they had made relationships top priority in their lives from the beginning, it would have made their lives a lot easier in the long run. Be sure to make relationships top priority in your life, and you, too, will be happier in the long run.

Number 3:

Relinquish the need to be right. That's it! Let go of the need to be right! It's sad, but most men would rather be right than happy. What happens is they get attached to being right, which creates disconnection, and then they wonder why they're so unhappy.

Did you know that in healthy, connected relationships, two people never have to fight? What do you mean, Michael? A relationship without fighting? That's not possible! Yes, it is! I can promise you that it is possible, and here's how: you must make the distinction between fighting and conflict. They aren't the same thing. Fighting is about being right. It's about being more concerned with being right than being happy.

On the other hand, conflict is what occurs when you bring two human beings together who will always have different opinions and beliefs. There's no way that you can avoid conflict in a relationship, but you can let go of your need to be right about the conflict, which will transform your relationships in an instant.

How many times have you had a fight over something really simple, and all you had to do was say, "That's okay," and let it go? But then there was a part of you that took this firm stand that you were just not going to let her be right. We've all done it. It's part of human nature to want to be right. Guess what? It doesn't work in relationships. Relinquishing your need to be right will transform your relationships in an instant if you will just be willing to let things go.

At the same time, there will be some things that you feel very strongly about, and you will choose not to compromise. You can do that without being attached to being right. You don't have to compromise your values in what's really important to you; you just have to be willing to say, "I don't have to be right. I'd rather be happy than right." When you do that, your relationships will transform immediately.

Number 4:

Be attentive to your partner. Being attentive to your partner means being in the present moment, fully aware of what they're saying, doing, and feeling. When we do that, we create a connection. When you really pay attention to your partner and you're really concerned about what they're saying, connection is created. If you really want to create healthy relationships, you must be attentive to your partner; again, it creates connection.

Number 5:

Express affection to your partner. That doesn't mean that you have to go out in the street and kiss your wife in front of a lot of people. Affection means that you're in some way affirming that you care about her by touching and acknowledging and possibly kissing her. Affection doesn't necessarily mean kissing; you can just touch someone and show affection. The key is to be comfortable making physical contact with your partner. Touching is a way to create a physical connection. Studies have shown that infants that are held and nurtured and physically touched are healthier than babies that aren't. It's in our DNA to be touched and held. Expressing affection shouldn't be a big issue unless you're stuck in your male ego, so let that go. Express affection to your partner.

Number 6:

Say I love you and mean it. If you truly love someone, why should it be difficult to tell them? When you say, "I love you." be sure to say it from your heart, not your head. Say it often, and mean it every time. If you don't feel it, don't say it.

Number 7:

Spend quality time with our partner. You have to define quality time, but quality time means you move away from all the hustle and bustle of life, the kids, the jobs, the house, and all of that, and you spend time where you're just hanging out. For some, it may mean just sitting on the back porch. For others, it may be going to a spa all day. You have to decide what it is, but it's important that you spend quality time where you're being attentive, where you're connecting with your partner. It's extremely, extremely important.

Number 8:

Loosen up, let go, have some fun. When was the last time you laughed with your partner? Just had a good laugh? If nothing comes to mind, something's wrong because relationships should be about fun, not just about stress and all the day-to-day challenges that we deal with. If you want to create a connection, you have to have fun because whether we realize it or not, we all have this playfulness inside of us. It's there. Too many of us have pushed it down so far, we've forgotten what it feels like, but we have to bring that playfulness back up and have fun and recognize that it doesn't make you less of a man to do so.

Number 9:

Celebrate your victories together. Life is tough enough as it is. Just look around you. We have all these things going on in the world. Our one refuge should be our relationship and our homes. When you accomplish something or something positive happens in your relationship, you should celebrate that. It can be something as small as a hug or something as elaborate as taking your wife out to a really fine dinner because she got a promotion at work. The key is to recognize that you're in this together and you should be grateful that you have each other. When you overcome hurdles, that deepens your connection. Have some fun, celebrate your victories together, and acknowledge each other for being there for one another.

Number 10:

Count your blessings, not your problems. Too many times, we focus all of our attention on what's wrong versus what's right with our relationships. When you focus all of your attention on what's wrong, guess what happens? Disconnection. If you're in a relationship, it may not be perfect, but you know this person is there for you, and that's something to be grateful for. Count your blessings for what she does right. An attitude of gratitude goes a long, long way in deepening your connection in relationships. Make sure that you're counting your blessings, not your problems. When you do that, I can assure you that connection happens and relationships bloom. That's just the way that it works.

There they are, The 10 Keys To Creating Healthy Relationships.

As men it is imperative we put more emphasis and focus on our relationships. We must make them top priority. Unfortunately, very few men are willing to put forth the effort in doing their emotional healing work that makes great relationships possible but since you're reading this book you are definitely not like most men.

Speaking for myself, my wife is the second highest priority in my life after my relationship with my Creator and myself. She comes before my children, my mother and my companies. She is my life partner and

I absolutely love sharing my life with her. She may not be perfect but she is definitely perfect for me and I count my blessings everyday for having her in my life and I will never take her love for granted. She loves me unconditionally and supports me in all of my dreams and goals and I'm truly blessed to be able to share everything with her.

I want to close this chapter with something I wrote back on Saturday, May 15th 1993 at 8:06pm. I had made up my mind that I wanted to find my Soul Mate so I decided to put my vision on paper so I would be clear on what I was looking for. Six years later I found her and on April 9th 2002 I married the love of my life and I've been blissfully married ever since.

Since I was able to find the love of my life I am absolutely certain you can too. So after reading my vision if you happen to be single, be sure to write your own vision and then commit to finding the person of your dreams.

They're out there! You simply have to be willing to do your inner work so you can attract them into your life.

Good luck!

MY SOUL MATE

My Soul-Mate will be intelligent, physically fit, spiritual and complete within herself. She will be able to receive all the love I have to give and also able to give her love freely. She will be confident and centered and able to allow me the freedom to be who I am, and I will do the same.

My Soul - Mate will be emotionally honest and trustworthy and willing to become one with her spiritual equal.

Together we will grow and expand and support each other in becoming all we were created to be.

She will have a great sense of humor and we will spend hours just laughing and giggling and being silly.

*We will take life sincerely, but not seriously.
She will love children and accept my children as her own.*

We will vow to make our relationship a commitment to God and therefore create a bond that can never be broken.

Everyday will be an acknowledgement of how fortunate we are to have each other and we will be committed to growing our relationship through eternity.

We will experience lovemaking at the deepest most intimate level possible and each encounter will be an expression of our deep love for one another.

We will travel the world together and experience all the wonders of God's great creation called earth.

It will be the joining of two complete souls coming together to unite in the love of God!

To keep the body in good health is
a duty...
otherwise, we shall not be able to
keep our mind strong and clear.

          Buddha

LESSON SIX:
Health

When I was 18 years old I suffered a heart attack. Technically it wasn't really a heart attack but it may as well have been. Here's what happened.

I woke up one morning as usual and jumped in the shower to get ready to go to work. As I was rinsing off I felt a slight tightness in my chest. It felt like the beginning of a muscle cramp. I ignored it and continued to get ready for work. After getting dressed I got in my car and drove to work and forgot all about the tightness in my chest.

At the time, I was working for a building material company and one of my jobs was to fill up a lumber rack with 2X4's. As I was loading the rack I felt that tightness again and just like before I ignored it. I continued to fill the rack and then all of a sudden I felt a pain in my chest that felt like I had been stabbed with an extra large Rambo sized butcher knife. Then the entire left side of my body went numb and the pain was so intense that I blacked out and fell to the floor. When I regained consciousness I was on a stretcher and there were paramedics all around me. I had been unconscious for approximately 18 minutes.

As I opened my eyes I noticed my co-workers standing around with concern on their faces. I reassured them that I was going to be okay and the paramedics put me in the ambulance to take me to the hospital.

As we were driving to the hospital they hooked me up to an EKG machine to monitor my heart rate. Once the paramedic read the EKG report I remember him telling the driver to slow down because he said my heart seemed fine.

Once I got to the hospital they hooked me up to another EKG machine and the doctor came to the same conclusion as the paramedic. He told me my heart was fine. After reading the report the doctor asked me what was wrong and I replied, "you're the doctor, you should be telling me what's wrong."

He said based on my report there was absolutely nothing wrong with my heart and he had no idea why I had had this attack. He then started asking me questions about my diet and sleeping habits and when he did that a light bulb went off in my head.

I realized I hadn't been getting enough sleep. I had recently started this job and I was still trapped in a partying phase. So I would stay out late at night sometimes until 4 or 5 in the morning and still go to work. As a matter of fact a couple of times I stayed up so late that I would actually sleep in the parking lot for a few hours and then go to work.

After sharing this with my doctor he said everything now made sense. He said my body was so tired it simply shut down out of sheer exhaustion. He prescribed me some muscle relaxers and sleeping pills and I ended up sleeping for 21 hours straight.

After that incident, I had a new appreciation for just how amazing the human body is. I was actually amazed to know that my body was smarter than I was and it was smart enough to shut down since it knew I wasn't. Ever since that day I have taken good care of my body. I even became a personal trainer to gain a deeper understanding of how the body works.

Currently, at 58 years old I can honestly say that I feel as though I'm still in my 30's. With the exception of some bad knees from walking on concrete for 10 hours a day working retail and the occasional lower back pain, I feel pretty darn good physically. As a matter of fact I've already set an intention to live to be at least 100 years old and I'm confident I will make it and when I do it will be without medication or the aid of a walker. I plan on being fully active and able to get around on my own two feet.

There are several reasons for my optimism and expectation of living to be 100. First of all, I take very good care of myself physically. I do not smoke or drink, I watch what I eat and minimize putting "bad" things into my body, (although I love Taco Bell) I exercise, I meditate, I keep my mind sharp by reading and being a writer and I have a wonderful relationship with my wife, which fills my heart with joy. Combine these things together and I believe I have a surefire recipe for a long and productive life.

As men of color I believe it is extremely important to have a conversation about our health because some statistics suggest we lead the nation in most health related illnesses and death.

It truly amazes me how some men will spend time and money researching what type of car to buy or what kind of clothes to wear and yet they refuse to research how to take better care of their health. Therefore I would like to make some suggestions on what you can do to improve your health and hopefully inspire you to want to live a long and healthy life.

First of all, it's important to understand the human body is possibly the most amazing thing ever created by the Divine Intelligence that created this Universe. It is the only thing on the planet that gets stronger the more you use it. Contrary to what most people believe it does not have to deteriorate with age. If we are willing to put forth some effort and take good care of it there is no reason why we shouldn't live to be 90-100 years old.

Think of the human body as a vehicle that your spirit uses to move you around on this earth. It's important that you pay attention to warning signs that your vehicle sends you to let you know there may be something that needs attention.

Think of it the same way you think about your car. When the check engine light comes on in your car it lets you know that something is wrong and needs your attention. When you see the light you should take your car in for service to figure out what the problem is. Unfortunately, a lot of people will ignore the light and keep driving in hopes that maybe the problem will just go away. They keep driving until ultimately the engine fails and they end up spending a lot more money to get it repaired than it should have. If they would have taken it in as soon as the light came on it could have saved them a lot of money and time.

The human body works the same way. It sends us signals to let us know that something is wrong that needs our attention. One way the body sends us signal is our weight. Being overweight is the body's way of saying you are taking in more calories than you're burning off and therefore it has to store unnecessary fat in the fat cells to deal with the excess weight.

Another signal the body uses when there is a problem is high blood pressure. In order to survive and function properly, your tissues and organs need the oxygenated blood that your circulatory system carries throughout the body. When the heart beats, it creates pressure that pushes blood through a network of tube-shaped blood vessels, which include arteries, veins and capillaries. This pressure — blood pressure — is the result of two forces: The first force (systolic pressure) occurs as blood pumps out of the heart and into the arteries that are part of the circulatory system. The second force (diastolic pressure) is created as the heart rests between heartbeats.

Having high blood pressure can lead to things like heart attacks, stroke, kidney disease, loss of vision and even sexual dysfunction. The sad part is, checking your blood pressure is a simple, no cost, painless test and yet too many men of color refuse to take this very easy test. Unfortunately, thousands of men die every year from high blood pressure, which in most cases is preventable and definitely unnecessary.

Another signal the body sends out is high cholesterol. Cholesterol is a waxy substance found in your blood. Your body needs cholesterol to build healthy cells, but high levels of cholesterol can increase your risk of heart disease.

With high cholesterol, you can develop fatty deposits in your blood vessels. Eventually, these deposits grow, making it difficult for enough blood to flow through your arteries. Sometimes, those deposits can break suddenly and form a clot that causes a heart attack or stroke.

High cholesterol can be inherited, but it's often the result of unhealthy lifestyle choices, which make it preventable and treatable.

Lesson Six: Health

A healthy diet, regular exercise and sometimes medication can help reduce high cholesterol.

The only way to know if you have high cholesterol is by having a blood test. It is a good idea to have your cholesterol level checked annually to make sure your levels are normal.

These are just 3 of the warning signals the body sends out to let you know if there is something that needs your attention. If you will pay attention to your weight, your blood pressure and your cholesterol level and make sure they are in a good range there is a good chance you can prevent major health issues in the future.

The key to maintaining great health begins with making a commitment to an annual physical. Too many men of color die from preventable illnesses every year so it is incumbent upon us to minimize deaths by taking better care of our bodies.

Here is a list of 9 things from The Heart Foundation we can do to prevent heart disease and strokes and minimize unnecessary deaths.

1. Know your numbers. See a doctor to assess your heart disease risk factors and get regular checkups. Work with your health care provider to keep your blood pressure, cholesterol and blood sugar at normal levels. Blood pressure numbers of less than 120/80 mm Hg are considered within the normal range. Check your blood pressure regularly and notify your doctor of changes. A heart-healthy diet and exercise can help control blood pressure and blood sugar levels.

2. Take your medications. If you have high blood pressure or diabetes, your health care provider may give you medicine to help control it. It's important to follow your doctor's instructions when taking the medication. Tell your doctor if the medicine makes you feel bad. Your doctor can talk with you about different ways to reduce side effects or recommend another medicine that may have fewer side effects.

3. Eat a healthy diet. For heart, health doctors recommend following theMediterranean Diet. Eat more fruits and vegetables and choose foods low in sodium, sugar (especially processed sugars), animal fats and saturated fat. If you're carrying extra weight, focus on the quality of your diet throughout the day, not just during mealtime. Beware when snacking – certain snacks can add hundreds of calories to your diet. If you're thirsty, drink water instead of juice or soda.

4. Watch your salt intake. African Americans as well as adults aged 51 years and older and people with high blood pressure, diabetes, or chronic kidney disease should consume only 1,500 mg of sodium per day. **1500 mg** of **sodium** equals 0.75 teaspoons of salt. Most of the sodium we eat comes from processed and restaurant foods.

5. Get moving. Staying physically active will help you control your weight and strengthen your heart. Try walking for 10 minutes, 3 times a day, at least 5 days a week. This will give you a total of 150 minutes of moderate-intensity activity. If you live in an area that doesn't have a park or gym, look for ways to get in daily exercise at work or at home. Try going up and down a flight of stairs. Or walking in circles while lifting your knees as high as possible, can work your muscles and your heart.

6. Maintain a healthy weight. A big belly, compared to your hip size, is a sign of too much fat on your body. Pay attention to what you are eating and get plenty of exercises.

7. Teach your children. It is important for parents to teach children about the importance of healthy eating and regular exercise early on. Habits formed as children will carry on into adulthood.

8. Quit smoking. About 1 of 5 African American adults smokes cigarettes. If you smoke, **QUIT.** Smoking significantly increases your risk of heart disease. It's not easy to quit, but doctors have several methods that can help you kick the habit. Or call 1-800-QUIT-NOW today or visit smokefree .gov

9. Lower your stress. You can't always avoid stress in your life, but look for ways to manage your stress. Take a few moments each day to sit quietly and take deep, slow breathes.

The high rate of heart disease among black Americans arises from many factors, including unhealthy lifestyle choices, ingrained cultural preferences and attitudes, genetics, and socioeconomic and environmental factors. The good news is African Americans can improve their odds of beating heart disease by understanding the risks and by adhering to a preventative healthy lifestyle.

I TRULY BELIEVE that health is wealth. Therefore it's important to make investments in our health by following these simple guidelines. There are countless forces outside of us that we have no control over, like racism, discrimination, negative media stories and stereotypes. What we do have complete control over is our health. We and we alone are responsible for the food we eat and the lifestyle choices we make. Therefore we must make better choices regarding our health and wellbeing.

When it comes to health, it's important to remember that our emotional health is a contributing factor to our physical health. In other words, it's not what you're eating, its what's eating you that may be driving your behavior. When we feel good about ourselves on an emotional level we are more likely to take better care of ourselves physically. If we are struggling with things like addictions and feelings of inadequacy it makes it difficult if not impossible for us to truly be happy. If we aren't happy we really aren't healthy. This is the reason it is so important to make peace with your past and move through any emotional baggage you may be carrying. Unhealed emotional trauma will keep you from being happy and healthy so be sure to deal with any emotional issues as mentioned in chapter 2 The Cure.

Another thing I highly recommend is meditation. I have been meditating for more than 25 years now and I have to admit it is possibly the best investment I've ever made in my life.

There was a time in my life when I couldn't get my mind to shut off and relax. I would think so hard and so much I would get these massive migraine type headaches in which I could barely function. In an effort to alleviate those headaches I began a meditation practice. I begin by listening to ocean wave tapes because I've always loved the sound. The ocean wave tapes began helping me relax and I noticed that my mind begin to slow down and it wouldn't race around so much. After the tapes, I took a class in transcendental meditation, which helped deepen my practice and quiet my mind even more.

There is a general misconception that the purpose of meditation is to get the mind to go blank. That is impossible. The purpose of meditation is to make you aware of what you're thinking which then gives you the awareness to be able to change your thoughts. Most people aren't aware of their thoughts and thereby have no awareness of them. By slowing them down and paying attention to what you're thinking you can now control what you think, which will then change how you feel, which will then cause you to act differently. And when you act differently you create different results in your life.

Do yourself a favor and learn to meditate. You'll thank me later.

I also want to highlight the importance of exercise. Have you know the paradox that black men are stereotyped to be superior athletes and epitomize physical fitness yet black men lead the nation in most health related illnesses and death. Can you not see the paradox here? We dominate the major sports in America and yet by most accounts we are the unhealthiest.

We must reverse this trend and it begins with us taking better care of our physical bodies and this includes exercise and watching what we eat. It also means yearly physicals to ensure our bodies are functioning optimally and that we are feeling good and looking good physically. This also means abstaining from illegal drugs and substances and minimizing alcohol consumption.

Health is wealth so take good care of your body and it will take good care of you.

Stop fighting for room at the table.
Build your own table.

                                                                Tyler Perry

LESSON SEVEN:
Wealth

WHEN YOU HEAR the word wealth what's the first thing that comes to mind? For most people, their immediate thought will be money. Like most people, I used to think the same way. As a matter of fact I used to be so preoccupied with money to the point that it was all I could think about. I was obsessed with it. I read books about it, watched shows about it, and subscribed to magazines about it and of course I dreamed about it. A lot!

Back in the late 80's and early 90's there was a show titled Lifestyles of The Rich and Famous hosted by Robin Leach. I was literally obsessed with the show. It used to come on late at night and I would stay up late to watch it even though I had to get up early in the morning to go to work.

As I watched the show, I dreamed of one day being featured on an episode and having the opportunity to have lunch with Robin Leach. Unfortunately, he passed away so I'll never have that opportunity but I will always remember him because of that show.

One of my favorite magazines at the time was The Robb Report. It was a magazine targeted specifically to the super-wealthy which showcased the best of everything money could buy. Every month I would wait for my issue to show up so I could keep up with the latest trends and gadgets that only wealthy people had access to.

After some deep self-reflection, I realized that I've always dreamed of being rich. It began when I was a little kid playing in the woods pretending I was negotiating with J.R. Ewing from the hit TV show Dallas. He was my hero as a child and I simply wanted to be just like him. RICH! As a child I had no idea what he did for a living. I knew it had something to do with oil but I was clueless about how he actually made money. All I knew was that he had lots and lots of money and I wanted to do the same thing.

So I followed in J. R.'s footsteps and actually started my very first company when I was 14 years old. Obviously, I wasn't rich but at least I was moving in the direction of my dreams by becoming an entrepreneur. My first company was a janitorial service in which I cleaned motorcycle garages. I convinced an owner of a motorcycle shop to hire me after hearing him arguing with one of his mechanics about cleaning his garage. At the time the minimum wage was 1.40 per hour and I earned 5.00 per hour with my business. I ended up having 3 clients and it was my first taste of entrepreneurship.

When I got to high school I launched two other companies based on the two things I loved the most, which was music and car stereos. I bought some equipment and became a DJ and I did parties, dances and proms for high schools and individuals.

I also learned to install car stereos and ended up installing them for friends. I had a four hundred dollar car with a twelve hundred dollar sound system! Man, I loved that car!

After high school, I ended up getting a job with a multi-million dollar building material company and I let go of my small business ventures to climb the corporate ladder of success.

Because of my love for business and a strong work ethic I was able to climb the corporate ladder pretty quickly and became the youngest manager in the history of the company at that time. At the age of 23, I was living the American Dream and on the outside it looked as though I was successful. But as mentioned, my dream turned into a nightmare as I lost everything and had to start all over.

Losing everything was the best thing that ever happened to me. My divorce, bankruptcy and foreclosure challenged me to take a really hard look at my life and I discovered being driven solely to make money was one of the reasons for my downfall.

After healing the emotional traumas from my childhood I was able to see how my love for business is actually a part of my life's purpose and by losing everything I learned happiness doesn't come from money. True happiness comes from knowing who you really are and why you are here on this planet at this time. When you figure this out you can find true happiness and inner peace.

By losing everything, I learned to love myself just as I am and I learned I do not need any money or material possessions to be happy or to be loved. With this understanding, I am now ready to pursue my dream of one day becoming a billionaire by creating a company that positively impacts the lives of one billion people. That to me is what a true billionaire entrepreneur does. He figures out a way to help a billion people and in doing so he creates a billion-dollar company.

With that being said I wanted to share some of the other lessons I've learned over the past 25 years of my own journey. My hope is by sharing this information with you it might keep you from making some of the same mistakes I did and hopefully provide you with some insights to help you build a wealth of your own.

The most important lesson I learned is to not idolize money. As mentioned, I used to be obsessed with making money. In doing so I neglected the most important thing in my life, which was my family. Of course, I wasn't aware I was doing it at the time because I truthfully thought I was doing the right thing by working hard to become rich so I could give my children the things I never had growing up. The truth is I neglected my family in pursuit of making money and that was a hard pill to swallow at first. So do not make the same mistakes I made. Nurture your family. Be there for them emotionally and spiritually. Make your family your highest priority and never neglect them, especially your significant other. Make your partnership with your spouse/partner top priority in your life and always work together to achieve agreed upon financial goals.

The next piece of advice I'd like to share is to always have multiple streams of income. Do not just rely on your JOB to provide income. Find a side hustle or learn about investing. Always have more than one way to make money. This also means you learn the basic tenet of gaining wealth which is to make sure you always have more coming in than is going out. In other words, learn to save money. The key to building wealth isn't about how much you make, rather, it's about how much you spend. When you learn to spend a lot less than you make you are on the road to building wealth.

The next tip is to always maintain good credit. Too many times we take this for granted and we overspend and wind up being in debt. Having great credit should be a safety net just in case you have unexpected expenses. Don't use it to try and keep up with the Jones's and live beyond your means. If you haven't done so join a credit reporting service like Credit Karma (www,creditkarma.com) that helps you keep track of your credit and your debt at no cost to you.

When it comes to wealth and money here is the best lesson I can share with you. It is absolutely okay to dream about making lots of it. But don't just dream about it. Take steps to acquire it. My suggestion is to dream big but simply do not make it a priority over your wellbeing and your family.

Throughout this book, I've talked a lot about the power of beliefs and without question, your beliefs about money will dictate how much you will or will not make.

I am going to share some wisdom from a man named T. Harv Eker. He is the author of the New York Times best- selling book, Secrets of The Millionaire Mind.

"Having the right set of beliefs that support your success and financial freedom is critical to achieving your life's desires. But most people have non-supportive, fear-based beliefs about money, wealth and success that were developed by modeling influencers like parents, friends, teachers, the media and even the web."

The good news is that beliefs are neither right nor wrong – they are only beliefs – which means you can change them if you want to. If a belief is not helping you, simply replace it with one that does."

This is your key to unlocking the door to building wealth. You must first challenge your deeply held beliefs about money and if they aren't serving you, then you must be willing to change them.

So, I'm going to list 10 fear-based beliefs T. HarvEker shared and a lot of people believe and hold on to. As long as you're holding on to

Lesson Seven: Wealth

these beliefs it will impact your ability to bring money into your life. So, take a moment to read this list and see if you're holding on to any of these fear-based beliefs.

1. I have to work hard for money
2. Money is a limited resource
3. I can't control if I become wealthy or not
4. It takes a lot of money to start a business
5. Money can't buy me happiness
6. More money means more problems
7. Money is the root of all evil
8. I never have any extra money
9. I can either make money or do what I love, not both
10. It's not right to be rich when so many other people are poor

Now, I want you to be completely honest with yourself and underline the beliefs from this list you may have been holding on to. The key to changing any belief is to first acknowledge you have it. So, go ahead and underline any of the fear-based beliefs you may have.

And now I want you to read this list of millionaire beliefs and then replace the fear-based ones with these.

1. I do what I love, I solve problems, and I make a large profit
2. There's enough money for everyone who is willing to earn it
3. I create my life and take consistent actions to make it how I want it
4. Starting my own business will allow me to have no limits on my income
5. Money gives me the freedom to do things to improve my quality of life
6. More money means more choices in every aspect of my life
7. Money is a resource to do good in my life and for others
8. I manage my money because when I do, more money comes my way
9. I don't have to choose between making money and pursuing my passion. I can do both.
10. I can do more for others when I'm rich than when I'm broke

Changing deeply held beliefs can be challenging, but rest assured you can do it. One way to do it is by using the Mirror Technique. Simply stand in front of a mirror and repeat each millionaire belief out loud to yourself. It's important you pay attention to how you feel as you say them to ensure you change them. As you say them, simply notice how you feel. If you feel a little timid at first that's okay. But make sure you get to a point where you are not only comfortable saying them, but you also have a deep conviction that they are true for you. It might take several attempts to change them, but you will feel a shift inside yourself when the belief changes. Do this on a regular basis and I can assure you your attitude and your flow of money will change.

Once you identify your fear-based beliefs and change them, then you must learn to pay attention to the synchronistic events that will start to occur. This is based on spiritual principles and at the beginning might feel a little irrational. It's important you learn to trust Infinite Intelligence and trust has nothing to do with what you think - it has everything to do with how you feel. This is why it's so important to trust your inner wisdom. As Master Yoda so succinctly stated, "You must feel The Force." I'll say this again: having faith and trusting the Universe has very little to do with what you think. It has everything to do with how you feel. Knowing is a feeling. It is the complete absence of doubt. You may not fully understand it, but intuitively you must learn to trust it.

Once you begin changing your deepest beliefs about money you will begin to notice coincidental synchronicities that begin to show up in your life. Remember, Infinite Intelligence works in mysterious ways so you simply have to learn to pay attention to the little nudges the Universe will begin sending you.

To make a point, I want to share a story that happened to me several years ago when I was trying to raise money to start a non-profit business idea I had.

More than twenty years ago I had a dream to run a company that would develop self-esteem building programs for children. I had no experience in developing programs and I had no idea how to start a non-profit organization that would implement these programs. Despite my lack of knowledge and experience, I decided that I would start a company anyway. After several years of failure I held on to my dream of building this company, but the reality was my life had actually fallen apart. I got to a point where I was homeless for a couple of years, and despite the challenges I still held on to the dream.

Approximately seven years after I had conceived the idea for my company, I had no luck in getting it funded. Despite this, I held on to my dream and continued to look for ways to bring my dream to reality. During this time I was renting a rundown one-room apartment and I was making minimum wage working at a video store. I had a bicycle for transportation and I could barely make ends meet. But somehow I intuitively knew that I would eventually figure out a way to raise the money for my company.

One day while working at the video store, a man came in with his children and asked me if I could make a recommendation for some movies for them to watch. I made the recommendation and he took them home to view them with his children.

A couple of days later he came back and told me that his children absolutely loved the movies and he wanted to thank me for the recommendations. He then became a regular customer that would always come in on the weekends and pick up movies to watch.

One evening he came in and we started talking, and somehow we began talking about challenges in life. He then told me that he was dealing with a major challenge because he had recently been diagnosed with cancer. During our conversation, I mentioned some of the challenges I had gone through, and I suggested to him that no matter how difficult challenges might be, there is always a positive lesson for us to learn within them.

When I said that, he smiled at me and said he completely agreed. He told me how his diagnosis had challenged him to really take a deep look at his life, and since he had been diagnosed he had actually been happier with his life because for the first time he realized just how important his children were and how precious his life was. As a result of his cancer he had become a better father, and ultimately a better man.

After our conversation, we became close friends and each time he would visit we would spend some time just chatting and supporting each other.

One day I was at work with a co-worker and my friend came in and asked for some movie recommendations. After he picked up his movies and left, my co-worker asked me if I knew who he was. I told him yes, and said that he was a friend of mine. My co-worker then asked me again,

"Do you realize who that is?" I said yes, his name is Mike and he is a good customer and a good friend of mine.

My co-worker then informed me that he was a very wealthy businessman who owned an oil company.

The next time my friend came in the store I decided to ask him if he might be able to help me with my dream. I told him about my dream of creating the programs for kids and I asked him if there was any way that he could help out.

He then reached into his pocket and handed me one of his business cards. "Michael, whatever you're working on I would be glad to help you. Contact my secretary and make an appointment and let me see what I can do."

During this time I was deeply involved with spiritual teachings and I had learned to keep my heart and my mind open to miracles. I didn't know how he would help me, but I intuitively knew that somehow he would.

A few days later I met him at his office and I was pleasantly surprised to learn just how wealthy he was. His office was like something you would see on a television set. It was filled with sports memorabilia, wild animals, and pictures of my friend with former presidents and lots of famous celebrities.

I sat down and began explaining my idea to him. After I finished, he picked up the phone and contacted another wealthy businessman who was in charge of a non-profit foundation that had access to lots of money. He told the person on the phone that I would be coming by to visit him and that he wanted to make sure that he would support my programs.

When he hung up the phone he gave me another business card and told me to make an appointment to see the guy he had just spoken with, and he assured me that the man would be able to help me in some way. I thanked him repeatedly and let him know just how much I appreciated his support. He then looked at me and said *"I want to thank you for being my friend and for listening to me and sharing your dreams with me. I believe you are going to be very successful and I'm glad that I was able to help."*

A few weeks later I met with the other businessman who loved my business idea, and a few months later I received a check for fifty thousand dollars to get my company started.

Let that sink in for a moment. I was completely broke, I had no formal education or training, I had a bicycle for transportation, and I was living in a rundown dilapidated apartment that I could barely afford. Despite all of these challenges, I was able to receive a check for fifty thousand dollars!

A lot of people would say that this was just a coincidence or I was just lucky. I, on the other hand, recognize that this had absolutely nothing to do with luck. It was divine synchronicity that orchestrated all of the events that led to me receiving the funding. It began with my belief that I would receive the funding. Faith is defined as evidence of things unseen, and I had unwavering faith that somehow I would be able to secure funding. It was then followed by my willingness to work extremely hard to keep my head above water while I was trying to start my company.

My faith and belief in The Source and myself gave me the patience and persistence to not give up even after several years of failure. The key was my willingness to listen to my intuition and to trust that The Source would provide me with the guidance I needed to be at the right place at the right time to meet the right people. By relying on The Source 100% and being willing to combine action with faith, I was able to locate the funding to get my company started.

This is why it is so important to learn to listen to, and trust, your intuition. As I've mentioned, The Source is constantly communicating with us through our intuition, and when we tune in and learn to connect the dots of synchronicity, The Source can guide us to our ultimate destiny.

So learn to listen to your heart and connect to your intuition, and you will receive all the guidance you need to live the life of your dreams and build any amount of wealth you would like.

I'm a living proof of this.

"For me, spirituality is the moment to moment recognition and acknowledgement of my connection to something greater than myself."

Coach Michael Taylor

LESSON EIGHT:
Spirituality

I WOULD LIKE TO ask you a very important question. As a matter of fact, it's possibly the most important question you've ever been asked. So when I ask the question I want you to take a moment and truly think about it before you answer. Spend some time in deep contemplation and then answer the question as honestly as you can. Try not to allow other people's opinion or what you have been taught to believe to influence your answer. Listen to your own heart and mind and answer truthfully. No one needs to know your answer except you.

Are you ready?

What are your beliefs about God?

Notice I didn't ask you if you believe in God, I asked what are your beliefs about God. For some people, they may not believe God exists. For other people they may have a very strong belief in God. Some may believe in an anthropomorphic god sitting in heaven taking notes of their lives and waiting for them to die to see if they are able to get into heaven. Others may believe in a God of love who loves them unconditionally and accepts them with open loving arms and showers them with grace.

So if you truly want to know what type of God you believe in let me suggest you simply take a deep look at your life right now and you will find your answer. As I mentioned earlier, your belief about a thing creates your experience of that thing. So if you believe in an angry judgmental God to whom you have to repent of your sins to try and get into heaven, chances are your life is filled with fear and anxiety. On the other hand, if you believe in a God of love then your life could be filled with joy, inner peace and happiness.

But ultimately your beliefs about God will always create your experience of God so it's important to be really clear about what you believe. I am convinced most people really do not know what they believe about God. They may know what they were taught to believe about God through their families and their cultures but they have never really questioned or challenged those beliefs. They have simply accepted beliefs that may have been passed down for generations and they are absolutely convinced that their beliefs are the "right" beliefs and anyone who doesn't believe what they believe is "wrong".

My intention with this chapter isn't to convince you that God exists. My goal isn't to try and change your mind about what you believe about God. My intention is to share my own journey to find a connection with a power greater than myself. I'm definitely not saying this is "the Truth" about God; I'm simply sharing "my Truth" about God. My truth is just that, it's my truth and what I have come to believe about God after a 25-year search that culminated into an intimacy and connection with a power greater than myself that defies human comprehension. This connection and intimacy drives my entire life. Everything I do is based on my belief that there is a power greater than myself in the Universe that I have direct access to and this is why my definition of spirituality is "the moment to moment recognition and acknowledgement of my connection to something greater than myself".

My hope in sharing my journey is that I share some fuel for contemplation that challenges you to ask yourself some deeper questions about God that ultimately guides you to find your own truth. I want you to experience what it feels like to "know" with every fiber of your being that there is a power greater than yourself which you have access to and when you access it nothing is impossible for you.

Now, if you're ready to dive in, let's get started!

When I was 6 years old my oldest sister became extremely ill. My mom was a single mother with 6 kids and because of my sisters illness, she decided to send me, one of my brothers and one of my sisters to live with our father. Coincidently, my father lived with his mother who turned out to be the grandmother from hell.

Lesson Eight: Spirituality

When I was approximately 10 years old I remember going to Rising Star Baptist Church in LaMarque, Texas. I remember it vividly because I really hated going to church. Even at the age of ten, I had tons of questions about God that no one would answer which led me to feel frustrated and angry and that's probably the reason I didn't like going. If someone would have taken the time to answer some of my questions my attitude would have possibly been a lot different.

One day my grandmother asked me if I wanted to be baptized and my immediate response was an emphatic no! I really disliked everything about the church so why in the world would I want to be baptized in it? Even more importantly, I didn't want to be baptized because I had no idea what it meant. I had seen other children being baptized but I still couldn't figure out what the point of it was.

Of course, my grandmother demanded that I do it and she would not take no for an answer. Even as a child I noticed the hypocrisy in forcing me to do something I didn't want to do. My grandmother was my primary caregiver who insisted that I go to church even though she did not go herself. In addition, she was a raging alcoholic who took her rage and anger out on me with physical and verbal abuse and in no way did she model this loving God she was forcing me to accept. I hated her and I hated her God.

When it came time for me to be baptized I was terrified. A part of me was afraid the minister might intentionally drown me because I was told I was a sinner and I thought to myself maybe God really didn't like me. Fortunately, he didn't murder me and I survived. But I didn't feel any different after the baptism. I had heard testimonies from people about feeling the Holy Spirit after their baptism but I felt nothing. If anything, I felt happy I didn't drown.

After my baptism, I was forced to be more active in the church. I had to go to vacation bible school and I even served as an usher. Every Sunday was the same routine. Get up, have breakfast, go to early morning services, come home and have lunch then go back to church for evening services.

I hated it! It simply did not make sense to me.

This went on for 7 excruciating years. After 7 years I was finally reunited with my mom and was able to leave. I can't express in words the joy I felt when I left my grandmother and that church but I will say it felt like leaving hell and going to heaven.

Although my mother was religious and went to church she didn't force me to go to church the way my grandmother did. Even though I still had doubts about the existence of God I was so happy to be back home with her that I voluntarily went just to be with her.

My attitude about God begins to change when my mother introduced me to her boyfriend Al. Al was an intelligent and thoughtful man who would actually listen to my questions about God and then share his ideas and opinions with me. He would occasionally go to church with us and after the service he and I would have deep discussions about what was said in church that day. He was a nonjudgmental sounding board that allowed me to express my authentic thoughts and feelings about God and I loved and respected him for his willingness to not only listen but also share his beliefs with me.

One of the most powerful lessons he shared with me came after a Sunday service in which the minister declared that the only way to get to heaven was through accepting Jesus Christ as your Lord and savior. All my life I had heard this message from the ministers and yet deep down I simply didn't believe it was true. To me it was irrational. It simply didn't make sense. Why would an all-powerful God set up a system in which everybody had to believe the same thing and if they didn't believe the same thing why would they be banished to this fiery furnace called hell? What kind of God would want to see the children he was supposed to love burn in hell? Why not just kill them off and be done with it?

So Al and I were having a discussion about this and this is what he said. "I do not believe that heaven and hell are geographical locations. They are really just states of consciousness. I believe in a God of love who accepts us unconditionally. The God I believe in never punishes us or condemns us because God is love, and therefore that is all he can do, love us. I believe there are many different paths to god and it is up to us to find the path that is right for us and ultimately all paths lead to

Lesson Eight: Spirituality

the same place. God goes by many different names but ultimately God is simply a word we use to try and comprehend the incomprehensible."

After that conversation I no longer hated God but I did want to try and find the path that was right for me.

Once I grew up and moved out on my own I didn't think about God much. I was caught between being an Atheist and Agnostic so I didn't attend church. I worked really hard and as I've mentioned I climbed the corporate ladder and by the age of 23, I was living the American Dream. At the age of 29, that dream turned into a nightmare as I experienced divorce, bankruptcy, foreclosure and a deep state of depression.

In an attempt to alleviate the pain I was in I decided to go back to church. Since I was brought up Baptist I found a Baptist church and started to attend on a regular basis. The minister was a lot different than the minister from my childhood. He was much more positive and uplifting and he actually inspired me. I actually enjoyed going to church for a while.

But after a couple of months, the questions from my childhood kept creeping up. I still had a lot of unanswered questions that needed to be answered and those questions were like a splinter in my mind that I couldn't remove.

One night I was sitting up late because there was a question that had been bugging me for my entire life. I kept asking myself this question over and over in my mind and I needed the minister to answer it for me.

The next Sunday I asked the minister if I could speak with him after the service. He agreed and after services, we met in his office. I told him I had a question I needed to ask him and his answer to the question would determine whether or not I would stay with his church.

He looked a little confused but he assured me he would answer the question to the best of his ability.

I then posed this hypothetical question to him. " I want you to imagine there are two men who are born at exactly the same time under two completely different circumstances. One man is born into extreme wealth and the other is born in abject poverty. Now imagine the man who is born into poverty becomes a criminal. He robs and steals and possibly even takes someone's life. On the other hand, the person who is born into wealth is a model citizen. He feeds the hungry, shares his wealth and by all intents and purposes, he is a good man.

Now imagine they die at exactly the same time and they both wind up at the entrance to heaven. Standing at the gate is God Almighty and he is standing behind a podium looking at his book of life. God tells the man who was born in poverty to step forward and begins reviewing the mans life in his book of life. He then looks at the man and says "you have really done some awful things. But I am a God of love and forgiveness and I have one simple question to ask. Do you or did you accept my son Jesus Christ as your Lord and savior?"

The man looks up at God and says, God, I have made a lot of mistakes in my life and I am truly sorry for them. I repent of my sins and I accept your son as my lord and savior.

God smiles at the man and allows him to enter into heaven.

Next, he calls up the man who was born into wealth. He begins reviewing his life and a large smile comes across his face. He looks at the man and says: "you have been a wonderful and loving human being. You epitomized me in every way possible. Your actions have been admirable and now all I need to hear from you is that you accepted my son as your lord and savior and then I can welcome you into heaven."

The man looks up at God with some trepidation and then he says; " well God there is a small problem. I can't accept your son as lord and savior because first of all, I've never even believed that you even existed."

So God looks at the man and then tells him he will have to spend an eternity in hell and he sends the man off to hang out with Satan.

So after sharing this hypothetical story, I asked the minister if that was how his God works. Without hesitation he looked me straight in the eye and said yes, that is what the bible teaches and that is what he believed.

In that moment, years of anger and frustration surfaced and I looked at the minister and respectively asked him; "are you out of your mind? That is the most irrational belief I've ever heard. How in the world can you believe that nonsense? I tell you what, I am willing to risk eternal damnation because in my heart of hearts there is no way that a loving God would ever do such a thing. I sincerely respect your beliefs but after this conversation, I am very clear on what I believe. There really is no such thing as God so from this moment on I am leaving your church and letting go of the idea of this fictitious being the world has created.

In that very moment, I became an Atheist. I walked away from that church and from God and I actually felt a deep sense of relief and freedom by making that decision.

After that conversation, I began doing research on Atheism. I became extremely comfortable with my newfound beliefs and I started focusing my attention on science and personal growth. I then came to the conclusion that science and rational thinking was all I needed in my life. As an Atheist, I didn't go around condemning or being judgmental about other peoples beliefs. As a matter of fact I did just the opposite. I was so comfortable with my beliefs I had no need to argue or defend them. Therefore I was very comfortable with opposing views about God because I knew exactly what I believed and allowed others to believe what they believed without judgment.

After a few years of being an Atheist, I became deeply involved with personal development and healing my childhood wounds. As I continued my healing process my life got better and I became happier but something was still missing that I couldn't quite put my finger on. During my healing journey, I began a practice of meditation in an effort to quiet my mind and feel more peaceful. My meditation practice led me to Buddhist teachings that began to change my mind about the possibility of God existing. During one of my meditations I had a profound revelation. I realized I had gone about it the wrong way. Rather than completely reject the idea of God, why not research God and come to my own conclusions?

This question led me to begin my search for the truth that would set me free. I started by researching the bible and gaining a better understanding of who wrote it and how it came to be. I was intrigued by how many different versions of Christianity there were and I took a lot of time studying exactly what Jesus said and how to use what he said to improve my life.

After studying Christianity I decided to research other religions. I spent a lot of time with Buddhist monks because of my meditation practice, and Buddhism was actually the first spiritual practice in which I felt something spiritual. What I love about Buddhism is it isn't really a religion. It is a practice of mindfulness, which is designed to help you connect with your Buddha-nature. Unlike Christianity, it doesn't preach that you have to do anything out of duty and obligation. There is no guilt or condemnation and you aren't seen as a sinner that has to earn your way back into the good graces of God. Even today I love spending time in Buddhist temples in quiet contemplation.

I also learned a lot of spiritual truths through the Bhagavad Gita and the Vedas and Upanishads from the Hindu religion. Hindus believe in multiple Gods (which I find fascinating) and there is sacredness about Hindu temples that I really love.

I went to a Jewish synagogue and learned about the Kabbalah and had one of the deepest and thought provoking conversations about life with a Jewish Rabbi. He was an intriguing fellow who like me, shared a deep love for science and he was able to incorporate science into his religion. I really enjoyed our talk and came away from it with a deep respect for the Jewish religion.

I was also deeply intrigued by a conversation I had with a man at a Muslim Mosque. I learned that Muslims actually believed in Jesus they simply didn't believe he was the Messiah or Divine Son of God. They acknowledge his divinity and miracles and even talk about him in their Holy Book the Quran.

After several years on my spiritual journey, I had a change of heart and started to believe in God. Even though I had spent a lot of time researching religions and concluded that all religions actually teach the same thing as Al had said, I was still mystified by the story of Jesus and wanted to learn more about his life. I then received a miracle that

Lesson Eight: Spirituality

would answer every question I had about Jesus and it would ultimately become the foundation of my spiritual beliefs.

I attended a personal development workshop called LifeSpring. During the workshop, I had a conversation about God with one of the other participants. She asked me if I had ever heard of a church called Unity and I told her no. She then told me that I would love it because it was a positive approach to Christianity and she said I was the most positive person she ever met and she knew I would fit right in. She even mentioned they were so positive that sometimes she didn't go because she was actually uncomfortable with so much positivity.

A part of me was a little hesitant but since I wanted to learn more about Jesus's life I told her I would eventually check it out.

Here is where the miracle happened.

The very next day I was at home sitting at my kitchen table looking through a phone book for something. All of a sudden my phone rang so I got up to answer it. When I got up I accidently knocked the phone book on to the floor. After I completed my call I picked up the phone book and when I laid it on the table and looked inside there was an advertisement for Unity Church. I smiled because I immediately recognized the synchronicity and jotted down the phone number to give them a call.

It turned out the church was only a few minutes away from where I lived so I knew I was supposed to go. I decided to drive by even though they were closed just to check it out. As I looked through the window of their bookstore I was pleasantly surprised to see books from some of my favorite authors regarding personal growth and spirituality. Now I was really excited and couldn't wait until Sunday.

When Sunday came around I parked out front and decided to see what type of people would be going in. I knew there would probably not be many black people attending because this was definitely not a traditional church setting. I decided to go in and I experienced another miracle.

There are some events in our lives that change the trajectory we are on forever. Some people would call them transcendent experiences while others might use the word divine. I'm not sure exactly what to call it but as soon as I stepped into the church something in me shifted. A part of me screamed with joy and delight as if knowing I had found my home. I could never fully explain it in words but the closest I can come to describing it is by saying I was bathed by a holy spirit. It was a palpable feeling of being touched by something divine. My soul lit up like a Christmas tree inside.

Once I walked in my suspicions were confirmed. I was the only black person in the church but it definitely didn't bother me because I was surrounded by nothing but love. I could feel the unconditional non-judgmental feeling of acceptance and it felt wonderful.

The first thing the minister said was it's time to begin our service with a meditation. What? Do they meditate in a Christian church? Is this real? I remember telling one of my Christian friends that I had begun meditating and she said meditation was trafficking with the devil. And now there I was in a Christian church meditating. Had I died and gone to heaven? It sure felt that way.

After the meditation, the minister gave a loving and inspiring sermon that opened my heart and filled me with the divine love of God. It was absolutely beautiful.

After the service, I was greeted and acknowledged for coming and of course they extended an invitation for me to join their church. Although I knew I would eventually be joining the church I declined their invitation so I could learn more about it. The experience was so new and different from what I was accustomed to I wanted to make sure I wasn't being pulled in to some type of cult or something.

So I grabbed some of their material and went home to learn more. During my research, I learned that Unity began in 1889 with Charles and Myrtle Fillmore. It is a nondenominational New Thought church that teaches a metaphysical interpretation of the bible that encourages its congregants to recognize that every human being has a spark of divinity within them and Jesus came to teach you how to access that spark.

Although I was impressed with what I learned about the church,

Lesson Eight: Spirituality

it wasn't the material that convinced me to want to join. It was that feeling I received the moment I walked in and it was my own inner wisdom that was guiding me to join.

During that time in my life, I was experiencing a lot of adversity and difficulty and I ended up having to move away from my home in Houston. I actually moved away to live with my brother because I didn't have a job and I had run out of money.

I moved to Austin and the first thing I did was find a Unity church. I started attending services on a regular basis and I committed myself to their teachings. One of their teachings is there is but one presence and one power in the Universe, God the good omnipotent and therefore if I am experiencing any adversity or challenge it isn't that I'm being punished I'm simply being redirected to something better. So despite my financial situation I accepted this truth and held firm to the belief that I was being guided to something bigger and better in my life.

Although it was difficult, I held firm to this belief for a couple of years before my life actually started getting better. But those challenges only deepened my faith and ultimately things started turning around and I was able to get back on my feet and move back to Houston.

Once there, I immediately found another Unity church. After the years of following their principles, I had developed my faith from just believing in God to knowing there was God. With this newfound faith, I decided it was time to fully commit to the Unity teachings by becoming a member.

But a part of me still had some negative residual effects from joining the Baptist church. I then decided that I would go and speak to the minister before I joined just to remove any doubt that I was doing the right thing.

When I met with the minister I told him the story about why I had left the Baptist church. I also told him that I really didn't trust preachers but since joining Unity my beliefs had definitely changed. He then said something that would put my mind at ease and confirm I was making the right decision. He smiled at me and said, "The most important thing for you to understand is I am no closer to God than you are.

You have the same access to God that I have. My job is to simply help you deepen your connection to God because that is where your inner peace and power will come from. Therefore your relationship isn't with me. Your relationship is directly with God." There was a calmness and sincerity in his words that truly comforted me. Unlike the experience I had with the Baptist minister, I had a deep sense of connection and sincerity with this Unity minister. A part of me knew I had found my church home and my soul was comforted by my decision to join.

From that point on I joined the church and I became truly committed to the Unity teachings. I took several courses and attended lectures to learn all I could about the Universal principles they taught. I even taught Sunday school to teenagers and even considered becoming a Unity minister but then decided against it because I came to the conclusion that I didn't have to be a minister to have a ministry. I then began my ministry by writing books and becoming a speaker who shares the wisdom and lessons I've learned on my own spiritual journey with others. I have now created my version of an extraordinary life and I am happier now that I've ever been in my life. Has it been easy? Of course not! Was it all worth it? Absolutely, unequivocally, yes!

As I reflect back over the past 25 years or so of my spiritual journey I am in awe of the grace and love of God. As I look back I can see how every adversity no matter how difficult or painful brought me a gift and a lesson that was for my highest good. If I had to do my life all over again I wouldn't change a thing because I now see the perfection in all of it. If I changed any part of it I wouldn't be the man I am today.

I mentioned at the beginning of this chapter that my intention wasn't to try and convince you that God existed. However, I would like to share a couple of truths that have allowed me to develop an intimacy and connection with a power greater than myself that allows me to know beyond a shadow of a doubt that God is real. I'm not asking you to believe what I say but I am asking you to simply contemplate these ideas and see if they resonate with you.

First of all it's important for you to find your own truth about God. Most people simply accept what has been passed on to them without truly asking themselves what they really believe. So my suggestion for

Lesson Eight: Spirituality

you is to honestly ask yourself what you believe and why you believe it. Be willing and open to the idea that what you may have believed in the past isn't true. Be willing to be wrong about God so ultimately you'll be right about God. In other words, find what's true for you. To do this you will have to challenge some deeply held beliefs but rest assured when you authentically find your truth it will be worth any discomfort you may have to go through.

Next, always remember there are many paths to God and just because someone is on a different path than you are doesn't mean they are the ones who are lost. Find your truth and allow others to find theirs. I can assure you if you will find your authentic truth it will not matter what other people believe and you will not feel the need to try and convince others that your truth is the truth. Find your truth!

Last but definitely not least, develop intimacy and connection to a power greater than yourself. Remember, the name isn't important, but nurturing and creating the connection is. My suggestion is to develop a spiritual practice that keeps you connected to this power and let me recommend that having a meditation practice is one of the best ways to create and maintain that connection.

In closing, my hope is that you have an opportunity to experience the unconditional love of a loving Creator. It is a feeling that is so deep you could never put it into words. It is like feeling the unconditional love of a child or being kissed by the beauty of a sunrise or sunset. It is joy, it is passion, it is reverence and love all rolled up into one thing. It is God and yet that word doesn't come close to expressing what it is. Skip the word and go for the feeling. Ultimately, it's even more than a feeling; it's the reality of the whole world.

I hope you get to feel it!

"We are shaped by our thoughts; we become what we think. When the mind is pure, joy follows like a shadow that never leaves."

Buddha

LESSON NINE:
Joy, Passion & Purpose

I ONCE GAVE A presentation titled Living With Joy. In the speech, I talked about the importance of having and expressing joy and I shared some of the reasons a lot of men struggle with being able to feel joy and express it.

After the presentation, a man walked up to me and said he didn't trust me, and he didn't believe what I said about it being possible for any man to find their joy. I asked him why he didn't trust me and he said his father taught him to never trust a man who smiles too much. He said men who smiled were always hiding something and therefore he had made up his mind that any man who smiled all the time was untrustworthy. He shared with me how difficult his life had been and commented that he had absolutely nothing to be happy about.

There was a lot of sadness and anger in his face and I felt a deep sense of compassion for him. I asked him if he wanted to sit down and talk a little and he agreed. I went into detail once again about all the adversities I'd been through in my own life and I shared my own emotional healing journey with him and how I had found my joy. As I shared my story I noticed he began to soften up just a little and I knew he was beginning to accept some of the things I was saying. By the time we finished our conversation, he was a completely different person. It was probably the first time anyone had really listened to him without judgment and simply created a safe enough space for him to get some things off of his chess. I was able to get him to see that he too could find his joy but he would have to be willing to change his belief about men who smiled. It was that single belief that had actually kept him from finding his joy. By speaking with me and finding out that I was sincere and trustworthy he was able to reframe that belief which opened the door to him finding his joy. After our conversation he even smiled and commented that it had been a long time since he had something to smile about.

As men of color it may seem as if we don't have anything to smile about. Once again, if we pay attention to the CWBS media it will convince us that the challenges we face are insurmountable and therefore there is no reason for us to smile or be happy. If you believe that you have contracted the "Illness" of a negative mental attitude and it is time for you to change your mind.

You must understand and accept that it is your responsibility to find your joy. You will never find it through mainstream media and you will never find it through a negative tribe. You will only find it when you become willing to do your inner work of uncovering any hidden emotional traumas you may have experienced and become willing to heal those traumas.

It goes back to what I said about energy. If you aren't feeling your joy it's because it is covered up with negative emotions. Maybe you're carrying around a lot of anger and rage. Or maybe your heart is filled with sadness. Whatever it is you will not access your joy until you become willing to heal that negative energy.

So the first step in finding your joy is to do your inner work and remove any negative emotions that may be blocking your joy.

One of my favorite movies is The Bucket List featuring Morgan Freeman and Jack Nicholson. In the movie, they play two men who appear to come from two completely different worlds. Morgan's character is a middle class mechanic who loves his family and enjoys playing Jeopardy. Jacks character is a billionaire who only thinks about money and the finer things in life.

It turns out they both have cancer and they end up in the same hospital together. Eventually, they become friends and Jack sees a bucket list that Morgan had put together about the things he wanted to do before he died.

Jack then decides to help Morgan complete his bucket list since

Lesson Nine: Joy, Passion & Purpose

he has the financial resources to do so. They end up going around the world completing the bucket list but most importantly they develop a deep connection and love for one another even though they came from different races and different financial backgrounds.

I don't want to give the movie away in case you haven't seen it (and I highly recommend that you watch it) but I would like to share a few of the lessons I learned from watching the film.

The first lesson was money couldn't buy happiness. Jack's character was a billionaire and had everything money could buy yet he was lonely and unhappy.

The next lesson was love transcends race. Although one character was black and the other was white their friendship transcended ethnicity.

The next lesson was about forgiveness. Jacks character had been carrying around a lot of anger and resentment towards his daughter and in the end, he learned how to forgive her and forgive himself which opened the door to reestablishing a relationship with the most important people in his life.

And the final lesson came from a story Morgan shared with Jack. The story goes there are some cultures that believe when you die and get to heaven there are two questions you have to answer before you are allowed to enter. Question 1. Did you have joy in your life? Question 2. Did you bring joy to others?

And now I would like you to answer those questions.

Once you can answer those questions affirmatively it's then time to find your purpose.

The purpose has been defined as; *"The reason for which something is done or created, or for which something exists."* I'd like to condense it and simply state, *"purpose is the reason that you have been created."* If you embrace the idea that there is The Source of all things (you can call it God, The Creator, or any other name that you're comfortable with), then try to imagine that The Source created you for a very specific purpose.

If you are truly committed to living a rewarding and fulfilling life, then I believe it is mandatory for you to discover your own unique life purpose. Without finding it, I believe something will always be "missing" from your life.

Before I share some insights on how to find your purpose, I need to begin by sharing why so few people ever find theirs. Although finding your purpose should be a high priority for all, the overwhelming majority will not take the time to discover what their purpose is.

The short and simple, yet complex reason most people never pursue nor find their purpose, is because our societal and cultural conditioning has always taught us to always look outside of ourselves for validation and fulfillment. Our media convinces us that materialism and the accumulation of "stuff" will make us happy, but ultimately this never works because happiness is an inside job and you will never experience it while looking "outside" of yourself. So the key to finding your purpose lies in your willingness to shift your awareness from looking outside of yourself to looking within yourself.

If you are familiar with the Christian teachings of Jesus he reinforced this idea by saying "seek ye first the kingdom of Heaven and all things will be given unto you." He then clarified what he meant by that statement by saying; "the Kingdom of heaven is within you." This kingdom can also be referred to as your interiority, which simply means the domain of your thoughts, feelings, and beliefs. In order to find your divine purpose you must be willing to become aware of this domain, and when you do, rest assured that you will enter the kingdom of heaven.

Although I stated, "Purpose is the reason that you have been created" you must understand that purpose goes a lot deeper than this simple statement. To fully grasp and understand what true purpose really is, you must understand there are actually two components to your life's purpose. The first is your inner purpose, and the second is your outer purpose.

Your inner purpose is your true essence. It can also be described as your "beingness", which is a set of qualities and inner attributes that make you uniquely you. Being intelligent, inspirational, creative, and

Lesson Nine: Joy, Passion & Purpose

compassionate are all expressions of your beingness. These qualities are always consistent with you, no matter what you may be "doing".

Your outer purpose or "doingness" is how you express your inner purpose.

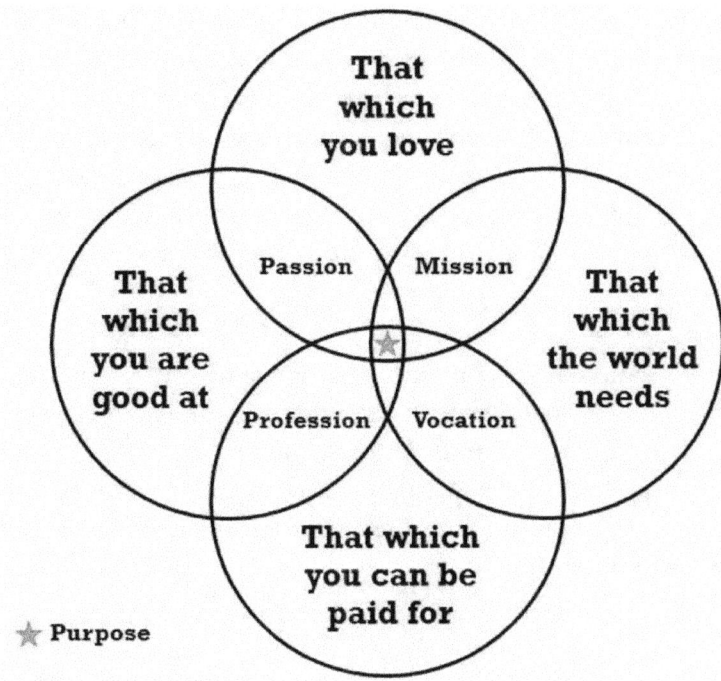

Take a look at this graphic. It shows exactly how to discover your outer purpose. If you begin with the top circle that says "that which you love" you have an exact starting point. In order to find your outer purpose, the first thing you have to do is figure out what you love to do.

If you go counter-clockwise to the next circle, it says "that which you are good at". This is extremely important in finding your outer purpose. It must be something that you are really good at. This is where some people get confused about their purpose. Here is an example; let's imagine that you love to sing, but what happens if you have a terrible voice that no one will enjoy? More than likely it means you haven't found your life's purpose; you've simply found something that you love to do. Just because you love to do something does not necessarily mean that it is your purpose. If it is truly your purpose I can assure you that it will be something that you are really good at.

As we continue going counter-clockwise, the next circle we get to says "that which you can be paid for". Getting paid for something does not necessarily mean that you are receiving money. Although there is absolutely nothing wrong with making money (and lots of it) getting paid for it means that you receive true fulfillment in doing what you love. In other words, you do what you love without the thought of compensation, but if you happen to be able to get paid for doing it that is simply an extra benefit. You aren't doing it for money, you're doing it because you love it, and when you do what you love the money will follow.

The final circle says, "that which the world needs". When you take what you love and combine it with what you are good at, and are then able to be compensated for your efforts and it somehow enriches the lives of others, you have found your true outer purpose. If you notice in the graphic, all circles overlap and meet in the middle, and that is exactly where you will find your life's purpose. If either part is missing you have not found your true life's purpose.

Another way to look at your life purpose is to think of it as your hearts desire.

Although every human being has a heart's desire, very few people ever find theirs. There are countless reasons why this is so, but one of the most important reasons is because we stop listening to our own hearts and begin listening to our rational minds. The reason we stop listening to our hearts is because a heart's desire is usually pretty irrational - it simply does not make sense. But when we awaken to our heart's desire it comes through as an inner knowing that defies logic, and that can be pretty scary. Some people may call it intuition, but it is knowing something without knowing how you know it. You just know it. You know it because it's in your genes. It's in every fiber of your being and it wants you to discover it. But the people who are close to you can't see it, feel it, or understand it, because it's your desire, not theirs. And

Lesson Nine: Joy, Passion & Purpose

they will do everything to try to protect you from pursuing it because to them it makes no sense.

Unfortunately, most people will not listen to their hearts; they listen to friends and family who will usually talk them out of their dream. The truth is, they aren't keeping you from your dream intentionally - in their mind, they are protecting you because they care about you. The problem is, you start believing them and not listening to your own heart, and pretty soon they have you convinced that you shouldn't trust your heart anyway.

Since most of us are taught to be logical thinkers and to always be cautious and safe, finding your heart's desire is extremely difficult. Society will tell you to go for the American Dream, which includes the house, the wife/husband, the 2.5 kids, and the 401K and you'll be happy. Get a good education, go for a safe career that pays the most money, and you've got it made, right? Wrong! It simply does not work that way.

Have you ever noticed how many people do all of these things and are still absolutely miserable? Why does this country have so many problems with addictions and medications? Why are so many people depressed and feel so alone? Why do 70% of people work at jobs that they hate or dislike?

It's because they haven't found their heart's desire. They haven't found their dream!

I don't want you to be one of those people. I want you to find your dream. I want you to find your heart's desire.

So I would like to share some of the lessons I've learned while pursuing my heart's desire and ultimately finding it. I'll begin by sharing one of my favorite books on the subject because it was definitely instrumental in helping me find my dream and unlocking my heart's desire. The book is *Building Your Field of Dreams* by Mary Manin Morrissey, and it is one of my all-time favorites. I highly recommend that you find yourself a copy. It is filled with incredible insights and inspiration that will lay out a step-by-step process for discovering and accessing your heart's desire.

The most powerful lesson I received from her book came to me during a time when I was basically homeless with no steady job or income and no car. Although I didn't have any material possessions, money, or titles, I had something more important. I had a dream. I knew what my heart's desire was and I had committed my life to bring my dream to fruition. But at the time, my life was a complete mess. I was in deep debt with no way of knowing how I was going to get out of it. All the doors that I approached to help get my company started were being slammed in my face. There were times when I even questioned my sanity because everything was going wrong. At times I felt like a complete failure because I had been pursuing my dream for several years, yet nothing had materialized. A part of me wanted to give up, but another part of me knew that I could never quit.

I began reading *Building Your Field of Dreams* and I couldn't put it down. I had been following Mary Manin Morrissey online for a while and I knew her philosophy and belief system about co-creation, so when I decided to purchase her book I knew there was a lesson in it for me to learn. As I was reading the book a sentence came up that I immediately knew was the reason I had picked up the book in the first place. It was the divine message that I was supposed to hear and when I read it, I immediately recognized the special message specifically for me. It said:

"All the while you think you are building a dream but the dream is really building you." That was it, my dream was building me! It all made sense. All the time that I had spent reading books and going to seminars to learn about myself and human behavior and personal development were shaping me to become the man I was born to be. All the pain and disappointment I had overcome was actually building my faith and preparing me for something bigger and better in my life.

As a result of pursuing my dream I had become better, stronger, more confident, and my faith was stronger than ever. As I sat there accepting the divine message in her words I began to weep. I was overcome with gratitude, and in that moment felt a deep sense of connection to something greater than myself. It felt as though God/Source was sitting right next to me comforting me and letting me know that I was on the right path, and there was nothing to worry about. I then knew that everything was going to work out and that I was definitely on the right track to fulfill my heart's desire. As I sat there with tears streaming down my face, I finally experienced the beauty of the famous poem called *Footprints in the Sand*. If you have not read it, I would like to share it with you now.

"One night I dreamed a dream.
As I was walking along the beach with my Lord.
Across the dark sky flashed scenes from my life.
For each scene, I noticed two sets of footprints in the sand,
One belonging to me and one to my Lord.
After the last scene of my life flashed before me,
I looked back at the footprints in the sand.
I noticed that at many times along the path of my life,
especially at the very lowest and saddest times,
there was only one set of footprints.
This really troubled me, so I asked the Lord about it.
"Lord, you said once I decided to follow you,
You'd walk with me all the way.

But I noticed that during the saddest and most troublesome times of my life, there was only one set of footprints.

I don't understand why, when I needed You the most, You would leave me." He whispered, "My precious child, I love you and will never leave you.

Never, ever, during your trials and testings. When you saw only one set of footprints, it was then that I carried you."

Chasing my dream had been the catalyst of my transformation. Although I began by chasing money and material things, I had now matured enough to recognize that it wasn't about the money. It was about me following my heart's desire and becoming the entrepreneur that I had always dreamed I would become, and to become the man that I was supposed to be.

I believe this is the reason why pursuing your heart's desire is so important. When you find your heart's desire and began to believe in it and pursue it, you will be guided to grow into the person you must become in order to fully materialize your dream. Every adversity, every obstacle, then becomes an ally for you. You begin to realize that that still small voice within you will begin to whisper in your ear, and you will hear the voice of your heart's desire and it will guide you to the places you need to go to fulfill your destiny.

So, let's begin the process of locating your heart's desire.

Finding our heart's desire can sometimes be difficult because of the factors I mentioned earlier. Our rational minds will sometimes keep us from finding it. Our family and friends will also keep us from finding it, and our cultural conditioning definitely plays a part in keeping us from finding our heart's desire.

The only way you will find it is by being willing to go within and discover it for yourself. This is an inside job that only you can do, so let me begin by sharing some things to think about that may help you find your heart's desire.

Since our heart's desire is encoded in our DNA and we show up with it, a great place to start is by thinking about the things you loved to do as a child. As children, we rely more on our feelings and imaginations than we do our rational minds, and if we pay attention to what Albert Einstein once said, it lays the foundation for finding your dream. Einstein once stated that "Imagination is more important than knowledge" and I believe he was absolutely correct in this assertion. When you search for your heart's desire there is a very good chance that it may seem irrational that you can accomplish it. A part of you will say that it isn't possible, while another part of you will say that it is possible. It's like having two sets of voices in your head. One I will call your rational mind, and the other I will call the voice of your Soul.

Your rational mind is the knowledge you've received from studying and observation, while the voice of your Soul comes from a much deeper and Divine place. The voice of your Soul is creative and unlimited. It is only limited by your imagination and your imagination is limitless.

So take a moment and think back to when the Wright brothers

Lesson Nine: Joy, Passion & Purpose

decided to create an airplane. Can you imagine how irrational that would have sounded back in their day? I'm sure their rational mind began trying to convince them that it wasn't feasible for a man to fly, but the voice of their Soul said something different. It said that it was definitely possible for them to create an airplane, so they listened to that voice and look what happened. Airplanes, space shuttles, Mars Rovers, were all created because two men decided to listen to the voice of their Souls and pursue their heart's desire.

Believe it or not, you are no different than the Wright brothers. You have a Soul voice within you that is constantly trying to get your attention. As a matter of fact, I believe it is your Soul voice that inspired you to read these words right now.

Do you remember pretending to be something as a little kid that really excited you? For me, I would pretend that I was a businessman and that I was negotiating multi-million dollar business deals in my multi-million dollar company. I even had a secret place in a wooded area close to my home where I would hold these pretend business meetings.

So what about you? Do you remember pretending to be a doctor, a rock star, a fireman, an athlete, an artist, a celebrity, or an entrepreneur? As you remember what you pretended to be, do you feel a sense of excitement inside yourself? Did thinking about it make you smile?

Or maybe you can't remember pretending to be anything as a child, maybe you currently have daydreams of something you'd like to become or something you'd like to have. Daydreams can actually be communications from your Soul that are trying to help you find your heart's desire, so it's important to pay attention to them because they just might be showing you what your heart's desire really is.

So, the first step in finding your heart's desire is to answer this simple, yet powerful and difficult question; *"What Do You Want?"*

As simplistic as it may sound, most people cannot answer this question because it's actually a lot deeper than most people realize. On the surface, people will say that they want to make more money, or they want to find their soul-mate, or maybe they want a new house or a new car. But if you are willing to go a little deeper, what you should find is a heart's desire that is wanting to be expressed through you.

Here is a simple exercise that can assist you in locating your heart's desire. I want you to complete this sentence;

I want.......

The key is to write down the first thing that comes to mind, no matter how irrational or absurd it may seem. Don't think too hard about it, just start free flowing whatever thoughts come to mind. Do not sensor it, just let the thoughts flow. Just keep writing until the ideas stop. If you need more space, get a separate piece of paper.

I want _____
I want _____
I want _____
I want _____
I want _____
I want _____
I want _____
I want _____
I want _____
I want _____

Once you've finished, take some time to see if any of the things on your list happen to be something you may have pretended to be, or pretended to have when you were a child. If so, pay close attention to that. Also notice how you feel as you review the list. If something stirs in you and you feel really excited about a specific thing on your list, you may have found your heart's desire.

Unfortunately, this isn't an exact science, and it may take some time to find your heart's desire. But if you commit to making lists of the things you truly want, and then listen to the voice of your Soul for the answer, then there is a very good chance that you will ultimately find what you are looking for. Stick with it until you do.

Once you find something that you believe is your heart's desire then you have to put it through the Mary Manin Morrissey *Five Essential Questions Test* to confirm that it's the right one.

I can assure you that if your dream passes these five questions you are definitely ready to pursue it as your heart's desire. Here are the five questions that you must answer to determine if you've found the right dream.

1. Does this dream enliven me?
2. Does this dream align with my core values?
3. Do I need help from a higher source to make this dream come true?
4. Will this dream require me to grow into more of my true self?
5. Will this dream ultimately bless others?

When I first read her book I immediately asked myself these five questions. As previously mentioned, I was completely broke without knowing how I was going to manifest my dream, but I intuitively knew that somehow I was going to make my dream come true. As I answered these five questions it confirmed for me that I was on the right track and it filled me with excitement and expectancy that I would fulfill my destiny.

Here are some of the insights I received when I asked myself these five questions about my dream.

1. Does this dream enliven me?

Whenever I would think about my dream I would light up like a Christmas tree inside. There was a passion and an energy that would surge through me at the mere thought of fulfilling my heart's desire. Even to this day, being an entrepreneur excites me and fulfills me in ways that cannot be explained in words. It's been said that if you do what you love, you'll never have to work a day in your life, and I can definitely verify this statement. I absolutely love being an entrepreneur, author, and motivational speaker.

As an author, writing is my passion. It is something that is in me. I literally *have* to write. While I am writing I enter this amazing flow of energy that I can't explain in words. Athletes call it being "in the zone" and it is something that is almost magical that defies description. As an entrepreneur, I am constantly challenged to ask myself deeper questions about how to run and improve my business. Though this can be challenging, it's one of the reasons I love it so much. I love the challenge! I am challenged to constantly grow and be creative in finding ways to make sure my business succeeds.

As you think about your heart's desire or dream, ask yourself honestly if it lights you up from the inside out. Does it make you want to get up in the morning? Does the thought of it excite you? The key is to be in touch with how you feel. When you find your heart's desire you will be filled with passion and energy that will become the driving force of your life. So if you do not feel this type of excitement and energy for your dream, you have probably not found your heart's desire.

2. Does this dream align with my core values?

Knowing what your values are is extremely important. Our values are the foundation of how we interact with the world, and they will definitely affect how we express our heart's desire. If you are unclear on your values it will be difficult to know when you've found your heart's desire. If your values include honesty, openness, fairness, and integrity, then your heart's desire will reflect those values. It's important that you are clear on your values before you seek out your heart's desire.

Imagine that someone says they share the values that I mentioned. They then decide that their heart's desire is to create a company that sells illegal drugs. Well, if their core values included honesty and integrity, do you think they would have chosen a company that does not embrace the values of honesty and integrity? Clarifying your values and making sure that your heart's desire aligns with those values are paramount to your success, so make sure that you're clear on your values and align those values with your heart's desire.

Lesson Nine: Joy, Passion & Purpose

3. Do I need help from a higher source to make this dream come true?

You do not have to adhere to any religious dogma or doctrine to accept that there is a power greater than yourself that can support you in fulfilling your heart's desire. As a former Atheist, I can understand if you have some resistance to this particular step. What I have come to know is that there is a power greater than myself in the Universe. This power goes by lots of different names, but ultimately the name is irrelevant. What's important is that you develop a relationship or connection with it if you truly want to find your heart's desire. Ultimately, you will have to rely on it to support you in finding and ultimately manifesting your heart's desire.

There is a wonderful quote that says, "If your dream doesn't frighten you then it's simply not big enough." Having a connection to a power greater than yourself will help you to move through your fears and will ultimately give you the courage, strength, patience, and perseverance to bring your dream to fruition. If you don't need assistance I can assure you that you have not found your heart's desire.

4. Will this dream require me to grow into more of my true self?

This is the true litmus test to see if you've found the right dream. As I mentioned earlier, all the while you think you are building your dream, the reality is your dream will be building you. If you do not have to grow to build your dream, then you are chasing the wrong one. Your dream will definitely take you out of your comfort zone, and that is one of the reasons you have the dream in the first place. Too many people stay trapped in their comfort zones and they are unwilling to get out of them. They are too afraid and unsure of themselves, so they play it safe and buy into the status quo.

My suggestion is for you is to get comfortable with being uncomfortable. There can be no growth without discomfort, so you may as well accept it. If your dream does not cause you to feel uncomfortable, it's definitely not your heart's desire.

5. Will this dream ultimately bless others?

Muhammad Ali once said, "Being in service to others is the rent we pay for our room here on earth." This powerful quote speaks to the importance of using our heart's desire to help make the world a better place. I personally believe that every human being has unique gifts and talents that are given to them to move humanity forward, and finding your heart's desire will unleash those gifts. When your dream blesses others then you know that you've found your heart's desire.

Finding your heart's desire does not have to be some grandiose experience that impacts the entire world on a large scale. Finding your heart's desire means you have found that special contribution that only you can make to the world. In your own unique way, you have had a positive impact on someone's life other than your own.

Your heart's desire could be as simple as baking pies for homeless people or teaching someone in your neighborhood to read. It does not have to be something that is featured in the headlines. It is simply something that you give from your heart unconditionally to another human being that makes them feel cared about and loved.

So instead of trying to figure out how to get rich or accumulate more material possessions, focus your attention on finding your heart's desire and I assure you will be rich beyond measure and more fulfilled than you can even imagine.

Of course, there is absolutely nothing wrong with making lots of money and having nice things. Just make sure that you find your heart's desire and do your part in making the world a better place, and everything else in your life will fall into place.

Good luck!

"If you want to go quickly, go alone. If you want to go far, go together." – African Proverb

LESSON TEN:
Find Your Tribe

As mentioned in previous chapters I was separated from my mom at age 6 and had to go live with my father and grandmother. I was there for 7 years and it was my version of 7 years of pure hell. During that time I experienced horrendous abuse and neglect. To deal with the trauma I became extremely studious and spent most of my time reading and being alone.

What saved me was a loving caring teacher named Mrs. Bussey who nurtured my love for learning and convinced me my intellect was my ticket out of the hellhole I was in. She knew about the physical abuse because I would sometimes come to school with bruises and there were several times when she had the school contact Children's Protective Services and filed complaints against my grandmother.

She and I had a very special bond. I remember her being slightly overweight because when I would hug her I would always imagine I was hugging Santa Clause. Her hugs were so warm and full of caring and love. Hugging was our little secret. She never hugged me in front of the class and I never told anyone else about them. She obviously knew about my abusive situation so she took it upon herself to shower me with love and attention when no one else would.

During my 7 years of hell, she became my surrogate mother. She was the reason I loved going to school and the reason I excelled academically. During my elementary school years I was a straight-A student. I also received perfect attendance at least 4 of the 7 years I was there in the hellhole. School actually became my refuge from the abuse, and having her there emotionally and psychologically was a lifesaver.

When I wasn't at school I spent most of my time alone. I didn't have any close friends and I always felt disconnected from my immediate family that I lived with. Although I lived with my father, we never developed any intimacy or connection with each other. Like most men back in the sixties, he worked all the time as a mechanic and didn't know how to emotionally nurture or support me or my other siblings. Although I longed to have a relationship with him like some of the families I saw on television, he was never able to give me the love and attention I so desperately craved.

To cope with the loneliness, I created a makeshift office in a wooded area across the street from where we lived. No one knew about this secret place because it was buried deep within the forest. It was a very special place where I was able to use my imagination and pretend I was a rich businessman. I had a makeshift desk and a large branch served as a couch and I would spend hours pretending I was doing business deals with my hero J.R. Ewing.

In case you don't know who that is he was a fictional character on a nighttime TV drama called Dallas. He was a conniving scheming rich oilman who was extremely popular back in the 70's. My grandparents loved watching the show and I would always watch it with them. Even though I had no idea what J.R. did for I living, I did recognize he was rich and I wanted to be rich just like him.

As I look back in retrospect I can see how my love for J.R. Ewing actually laid the foundation for me becoming an entrepreneur. I remember a conversation I had with my grandfather in which I told him when I grew up I was going to be rich. When he asked how I planned on doing that I told him one day I was going to own my own company.

When I was reunited with my mother at age 13 my dream of owning my own company was still fresh on my mind. At the age of 14 I launched my first company by convincing the owner of a motorcycle shop to hire me to clean his garage. I did such a great job he referred me to two of his other friends who also owned garages and I became an entrepreneur. In high school, I started two other businesses. I was a DJ that had his own equipment and I went around the city dee-jaying parties, dances and proms. Another passion I had was installing car

Lesson Ten: Find Your Tribe

stereos. I had a four hundred dollar car with a twelve hundred dollar stereo in it and it was absolutely amazing to listen to. There were kids from several different high schools who hired me to install their stereos so I made pretty decent money during high school as an installer.

When I was 17 I read the book Think & Grow Rich. It ignited a new passion for learning in me and it taught me I could use my mind to build unlimited wealth. After reading it, I made a commitment to reading business books and conditioning my mind to become a millionaire entrepreneur.

During this time I developed a friendship with 3 other boys from my neighborhood. We were inseparable. We played sports together, hung out at the movies and did all the typical things teenagers did together. Their friendship meant everything to me and I was willing to do anything for them. They were my family, my community or in todays marketing terms, they were my tribe.

Since my tribe was more important than my grades, I began skipping school to spend more time with my friends. Even though I knew my grades were suffering, the camaraderie and friendship I had with them superseded everything else. I needed to fit in and be a part of the group so I made sure not to do anything that would upset my tribe.

Although I spent a lot of time with my friends and was skipping school and watching my grades continue to plummet, I kept my commitment to reading business books. I never told my friends I was reading them because I didn't want to risk being called a nerd and possibly being rejected by my tribe. But I absolutely loved reading so I kept my love of reading hidden from my friends.

At the age of 19, I secured a job with a building supply company and got a taste of the business world. I worked extremely hard and climbed the corporate ladder pretty quickly. I became the youngest manager in the history of the company at the age of 22 and one of only two black men who had ever managed a store.

Once I became a manager I wanted to help my 3 friends I grew up with. Unfortunately, they hadn't grown up yet and were still trapped in a hustler's mentality and didn't want the responsibilities of an honest job with decent pay. They refused my invitations to get a job with my company because they said they didn't want to work for "the man".

I was really saddened and disappointed they wouldn't join me but it taught me a very valuable lesson about the importance of having a tribe. I learned you have to sometimes let go of people who you care about in order for you to pursue your dreams. I learned your tribe would change as you change. If you are on a path of success you must surround yourself with a tribe of people who are on that same path.

As men of color, finding the right tribe can sometimes be difficult. Speaking from my own experience, I have been accused of denying my ethnicity by belonging to tribes in which I am the only man of color. I have been called a sellout for joining a predominantly white church. (which is a tribe by the way) I have been called a sellout for reading books by white authors. I have been called a sellout for having white male role models and I've even been accused of being a sellout for being an optimist. So if you've ever had to struggle or deal with any of these issues you are not alone and the intention of this book is to support you in building a tribe where you can be yourself and not worry about whether you will be judged based on your own personal preferences no matter what they might be.

In other words, the intention of this tribe is to create a safe space where you get to be authentically you. A great place to start is on my website designed specifically to empower men of color to live extraordinary lives. The web address is www.shatteringblackmalestereotypes.com

On the site you will have access to courses, books, webinars and podcasts that educate, motivate and inspire you to reach your full potential. There are interviews with authors, speakers, psychologists, and former professional football players. It is an unlimited resource for any man who is looking for a tribe of like-minded brothers who are committed to positivity and empowerment.

So here is the reason tribes are so important. Remember when I shared how important my friends were? Remember when I said I would do anything for them? The reason tribes are so important is because as human beings we are social creatures. We are born to socialize and

Lesson Ten: Find Your Tribe

be a part of a group. Our first tribe will always be our families but sometimes our families are dysfunctional and toxic. Think about the relationship I had with my grandmother. At one time she was my primary caregiver yet she abused that responsibility by being a raging alcoholic who abused me. Therefore I never felt loved or connected in that family environment. When I created a tribe with my friends they accepted me for who I was and they loved and supported me unconditionally. They didn't judge me or attack me for any of my views or opinions. They were my boys and I loved them and they loved me.

However, it turned out that we had different dreams and aspirations and they were unwilling to break free from the environment we were in. Therefore I had to make a choice. Stay with my tribe or follow my dreams. I chose my dreams and I had to be willing to let go of my tribe. I still loved them and I missed them when I left but ultimately I knew I was making the right decision to move on with my life.

But it is still important to surround yourself with like-minded people who are headed in the same direction that you are. Your tribe should be your support system and cheerleading squad who encourages you and holds you accountable to the commitments you make. They should be the first ones you turn to when you need advice or encouragement. Your tribe should definitely lift you up and not bring you down. If your tribe is bringing you down it's time to find a new tribe.

I believe the most important tribe you will ever develop is your family. Your family should be your first priority in terms of tribes because your family should know you better than anyone else and they should always have your back no matter what the circumstances are.

For me, my wife is the most important member of my tribe. She is my highest priority. She comes before my children and even before my mother. She is my life partner and the only thing that comes before her is my relationship with my Creator. I put her before my company or making money and if I have to choose between the two I'll choose her every time.

Nothing comes close to the feeling of knowing someone loves you unconditionally. Not because of how much money you make or how much fame or money you have. They love you just for the wonderful human being that you are and they simply want to spend the rest of their lives with you. Just the thought of you brings a smile to their face and they will walk to the end of the earth for you. This is my wife and this is why I love her so much. She doesn't see me as an entrepreneur, author, speaker or radio host. She sees me as the man of her dreams who loves and supports her to be all she was created to be and she simply loves sharing this wonderful gift called life with me and I feel the same way about her.

So my suggestion to you is to make finding the right partner a very high priority in your life. If you're single reread the chapter on love and commit to finding your life partner. If you're in a relationship make sure you never take it for granted and take the time to deepen your relationship while strengthening your connection. Rest assured when you find the right one you will realize how important true love is and you will not settle for anything less. Start your tribe by choosing the right life partner.

The good news is, there is an unlimited amount of tribes you can join. If you are looking for a place to start here are a few suggestions.

First of all, you can begin with social media. If you aren't comfortable with computers and are a little hesitant about being online I suggest you move through that fear and learn how to use a computer. If you don't know how, you can go to your public library or even take courses at your community college. Having access to social media immediately opens the door for you to find a tribe to join.

There are countless options available for you and if you are new to social media. A great place to start would be Facebook. Facebook is a great resource for connecting with old friends and creating or joining a tribe. There are specific tribes for any age, race or interest. You just have to be committed to finding a tribe that you will enjoy being a part of.

There are tribes for black fathers and tribes for black entrepreneurs. There are tribes for single people and married people and they are always looking for members to join their tribe. There are spiritual and religious tribes and tribes for special interests like the group called Black Men Who Love Dope Cars. There are absolutely no limits to the

Lesson Ten: Find Your Tribe

types of tribes you can find, you simply have to make a decision that you want to join one.

On social media your tribe will be called a Group, so as you're searching, that's what you want to look for. Locate a group that interest you then simply click the add to Group button and almost instantaneously will you will become a part of the group. In some cases, you will have to be approved before you become a member but be patient and wait for the group to add you.

In order to be on social media, it's important for you to set up your profile. Your profile will let others know a little bit about you so they can see whether or not you have anything in common. So take the time to complete your profile because it will increase your chances of being accepted into a group.

Another place to find your tribe is with church groups. If you're religious and are looking for camaraderie the men's group at your church could possible work well for you. Join a group and build your tribe there.

What's important is your willingness to join a group and be willing to commit to sharing and participating within that group. Joining a tribe isn't like going to the barbershop where you are arguing and debating your points of view. Belonging to a tribe means you are willing to be open and supportive and nonjudgmental towards others as you work together to build the group. That is why it is important to find a group of like-minded people who have the same goals and values who are committed to accomplishing the same things as you are.

If you are really committed to joining a tribe but can't seem to find one that works for you, let me suggest that you start your own tribe. It may sound a little intimidating but if you're really committed you can do it.

Let me share how I started my first tribe almost 20 years ago.

I once read a book by Gary Zukav called the Seat Of The Soul. The book had such a positive impact on me that I wanted to go deeper and learn more from the author and his teachings. I began listening to some of his audio programs and watching his interviews on television.

I even had a chance to meet him at an event that was held at my church. During one of his interviews on television, he was asked how people could stay in touch with him and learn more about his work. He then mentioned he had put together a way for people to continue their growth with his work through something he called a Soul Circle. A Soul Circle was a discussion group in which people came together to talk about his book and to create spiritual partnership with other human beings. Anyone could start a Soul Circle and he put together a list of basic guidelines to support people in getting the most out of their Circle.

I must admit that Gary's teachings would definitely be considered nontraditional. As a matter of fact, there are some Christians who call his teachings blasphemous and anti-Christian. I disagree with that assertion wholeheartedly. I happen to believe in what he teaches and without questions, his teachings have enhanced my life so that is the reason I decided to start my own Circle.

After I decided to create my tribe I put together a little flyer and posted it at my church. As mentioned in the chapter on spirituality I was a member of a church called Unity and Gary's teaching is very similar to what Unity teaches. So the members of Unity are definitely open to non-traditional ways of thinking therefore I was comfortable posting the flyer about the Soul Circle.

The very first day I posted the flyer I received a call from a woman who said she was interested in joining. We met at a coffee shop and I shared my vision of the Circle with her. She was in complete alignment with my vision and she even offered to host the Circle at her home. A few days later a few other women called and we set a date to have our first meeting.

At our meeting, we decided on a structure of how the meeting would go and we agreed that we would never have more than 10 members. Within a few weeks we had our 10 members and the Circle really began to take shape and change lives.

One of the things I loved about the circle was each week a different member would choose a topic for the circle to discuss.

Lesson Ten: Find Your Tribe

It was completely voluntary and there were a few people who were really uncomfortable doing it at first but because of the supportive and nurturing structure of the circle, they were able to move through their fears and facilitate a circle. Challenging your fears is definitely a way to grow spiritually and each of us overcame different fears with the support of the Circle.

Sometimes we would talk about Gary's book and other times we would talk about other author's books. We had conversations about relationships, death, monogamy, God, sex, money and just about any other topic of discussion.

Another thing I enjoyed about the circle was we had a pink heart shaped stone that was placed in the middle of the circle. In order to speak you had to pick up the stone and then share. This made sure that no one side talked or talked out of turn. If you had something to say you had to wait until you picked up the stone and everyone adhered to this procedure, which made for very organized dialogs.

Occasionally we would open the group up to guests who might be interested in joining or even starting their own circle. It was a place that was committed to teaching people how to create spiritual partnership and without question, we accomplished that goal.

The Circle met once a week for more than 7 years. During that time I learned to trust and love the members of the group like my own family. As a matter of fact, they actually knew me better than my own family because I couldn't have these types of spiritual discussions within my own family.

After approximately 7 years we started meeting once a month and this went on for another 3-4 years and then we disbanded. So my tribe lasted for approximately 10 years and it was a powerful and transformational experience that I will treasure for the rest of my life. I am still close friends with a few of the members and our spiritual bond is as strong as ever.

Another tribe I was a part of was called the Virtual Men's Gathering. It was an online men's group that was held online through a video platform. Each week 6-10 men would meet through this online forum and discuss issues dealing with the changing roles of masculinity in society. There were men from Spain, The Czech Republic, Portugal, Canada, Norway and the United States. I was the only man of color in the group but that didn't matter because of our commitment to diversity and our commitment to doing men's work.

I was hesitant to join at first because I was a little skeptical about the effectiveness of being online but I was pleasantly surprised at just how powerful it was. At our online meetings, we would begin with a check-in. We used a format called a PIES check in which stood for Physical, Intellectual, Emotional and Spiritual. Each man would have an opportunity to check in without being interrupted by other members of the group. So when a man checked in he would begin by sharing how he was feeling physically, intellectually, emotionally and spiritually.

After the check in we would do something called a clearing. A clearing meant sharing anything that might be troubling you or keeping you from being fully present with the group. For example, if you had a fight with your spouse and needed the space to speak openly about how you were feeling the clearing gave you the freedom to do that. Once you did your clearing if you wanted feedback or advice then you could request it and any man could share his thoughts or feelings with you about your clearing. Everything was voluntary. You were never forced to share or speak.

After the clearings, we would then choose a topic of discussion for the meeting and we would proceed to have a discussion about that particular topic.

The beauty of a group like this with men who are truly committed to their personal growth is it challenges you to get real. In the group, you can't hide and be superficial because the men will bring it to your attention that you aren't being authentic. Because of our commitment to making sure you are being open and honest in your communications we hold you accountable to make sure you are being real. If you've never been in an environment it can be extremely uncomfortable at first but if you stick with it and trust the men in your group you can

Lesson Ten: Find Your Tribe

rest assured that you will heal and grow in more ways than you can probably imagine.

It isn't easy having these types of intimate conversations because as I mentioned in an earlier chapter men are conditioned not to feel. But in order to grow and heal, you must be willing to feel and that is the most difficult part for most men.

This is the reason men's work is so important. Men's work will provide you with the emotional tools to help you live a more rewarding and fulfilling life. Too many of us as men unfortunately do not have the emotional tools to create healthy relationships and to be happy with our lives and that's where men's work comes in. It gives you the tools to access the most important aspect of your life, which are your feelings and emotions.

I participated in the Virtual Men's gathering for a little over 2 years. It was a great experience for me and I highly recommend you consider joining a men's group to support you on your journey.

As I mentioned earlier there are unlimited opportunities for you to find your tribe and build a community of like-minded men. They are definitely out there but you are going to have to put forth a little effort to find them.

Just remember what I said at the beginning. Sometimes you just might have to let go of your tribe that is holding you back and find a tribe that pushes you forward. Make sure you find a like-minded group with the same values and intentions you have and then commit to building your tribe into a powerful and challenging network that propels you to a brighter future.

Find your tribe and build a life you will be proud of and don't forget the African proverb; "If you want to go fast go alone, if you want to go far go together."

Go far and go together with your tribe.

TAKEAWAYS

Now that you've completed the book, I'd like to share a recap of the things we've covered to ensure you grasped the messages from each chapter. It's important for you to review this information on a regular basis if you truly want to transform your life. It's been said "Rome wasn't built in a day" which points to the fact that change takes time, so you must commit to your growth and accept that change is an ongoing process and you must be committed to that process.

So let's recap the lessons from each chapter.

Lesson 1. The Illness

A negative mindset and attitude is an illness you must overcome. Remember you have complete control over your thoughts and actions so make sure you do not accept the CWBS stereotypes about black men.

Lesson 2.

The Cure is to be willing to acknowledge your humanness and discover who you really are. You are a man who happens to be black with infinite potential. Put another way; *"You are more than your thoughts, your body, or your feelings. You are a swirling vortex of limitless potential who is here to shake things up and create something new that the Universe has never seen."*

Lesson 3.

Embrace science and use it as a tool to support you in your growth. Do not rely on other people's opinions. Listen to facts and use them to your advantage. Be willing to break tradition and let science guide you to come to conclusions but at the same time trust your own intuition to guide you.

Lesson 4.

Understanding the roles of manhood and masculinity are changing rapidly for the better. Do not adhere to antiquated roles that keep you from being authentically who you are. You get to define masculinity for yourself so choose a definition that aligns with your highest truth.

Lesson 5.

Learn to love and be loved. Do not be afraid to open your heart and be vulnerable and compassionate. Make relationships a high priority in your life and find that special someone to share your life with.

Lesson 6.

Take good care of your physical body. Commit to annual checkups and stay away from ingesting anything that isn't good for your body. Learn to meditate and relax in addition to exercising.

Lesson 7.

Focus on building generational wealth. Create multiple streams of income and be sure to save more money than you spend.

Lesson 8.

Develop intimacy and connection to a power greater than yourself. Find your "Truth" and be willing to try different paths until you find the one that lights up your spirit.

Lesson 9.

Focus on finding your joy and purpose. Find the things that light you up and do that. Do everything with passion!

Lesson 10.

Create a network of like-minded people who will support and challenge you to become the best version of yourself. Stay away from toxic people and build a tribe of people you can trust.

I'd like to think of these as the 10 lessons to creating an extraordinary life. What do you think? Did you gain some insights to support you in doing that?

My intention has been to provide you with insights and inspiration to support you in creating a life filled with joy, passion and purpose. Was I able to do that for you? Do you feel inspired as a result of reading this book?

If the answer is yes, I hope you will share it with others. Obviously, there is no shortage of bad news concerning men of color so wouldn't it be nice if we began sharing some good news with each other? Here's your chance. Share the book with others. Create a group that comes together to discuss the content of this book. Use it as a resource for conversation and inspiration. Post it on your social media sites and share it with anyone who you think would benefit from it's content.

It's our time now. It's time for us to move past feeling like victims and become victorious! It's time for us to capitalize on the sacrifices our ancestors made which have allowed us to be where we are today. The future is filled with infinite possibilities for any of us who are willing to put forth the effort.

The question you must ask yourself is: "are you willing to put forth the effort?"

I'd like to close this book with a quote from Margaret Meade. This quote deeply resonates with me and I use it as a guiding principle in my life.

Think long and hard about it and then take action.

"Never doubt that a small group of thoughtful and committed citizens can change the world; indeed, it's the only thing that ever has."

I'm committed.

Are you?

RESOURCES

Here are a few resources if you're not sure where to begin to find your tribe. My company phone number is: 877-255-3588.

Email address: mtaylor@coachmichaeltaylor.com

Here are a few of my sites:

www.shatteringblackmalestereotypes.com

www.anewconversationwithmen.com

www.adversityisyourgreatestally.com

www.coachmichaeltaylor.com

Avante Branch is doing a fantastic job with the youth through their organization called The Ever Forward Club.

www.everforwardclub.org

Brandon Frame is on a mission to change the stereotypes of black men and he has launched The Black Man Can Institute.

www.theblackmancan.org

Freddie Weaver is an expert on sexuality and relationships. Check him out at, The Tantra Nova Institute.

www.tantranova.com

Jewel Love is a therapist who runs an organization called Black Executive Men and he facilitates a group called The Golden Rhinos.

www.blackexecutivemen.com

Brandon Alexander runs an organization called New Age Gents. His tagline is Building Better Men. Building A Better You. Be sure to check out his site.

www.newagegents.com

100 Black Men of America has been around since 1963 and their focus has always been about exposing men of color to positive role models. Their motto is "What They See Is What They'll Be.

www.100blackmen.org

BIO

Coach Michael Taylor is an entrepreneur, author (8 books), motivational speaker and radio and TV show host who has dedicated his life to empowering men and women to reach their full potential by transforming their lives from the inside out. He knows first hand how to overcome adversity and build a rewarding and fulfilling life and he is sharing his knowledge and wisdom with others to support them in creating the life of their dreams.

He is President & CEO of Creation Publishing Group that is a company that specializes in creating programs and products that empower men to embrace a new paradigm of masculinity that supports them in being great husbands and fathers and supports them in creating meaningful and rewarding lives.

He was featured in the Amazon.com bestselling book *Motivational Speakers America* with legendary speakers Les Brown and Brian Tracy and he has won numerous awards for his dynamic speaking style. Public speaking is his passion and being on stage brings him tons of joy.

He is the host and producer of two TV Channels on the Roku Network, *Joy Passion & Profit*, which is a show designed to empower entrepreneurs to build companies that change the world, and, *Shatter The Stereotypes*, which empowers men of color to live extraordinary lives. In addition, he hosts two podcasts of the same names and they can be found on most podcast platforms like Spotify and iTunes.

Most importantly he has been blissfully married for 17 years to the woman of his dreams and he is a proud father to three grown children whom he is extremely proud of.

When he isn't writing or speaking you'll find him checking out the latest movies or listening to old school 70's and 80's soul music and contemporary jazz.

He considers himself to be an irrepressible optimist with a passion for the impossible and he believes there has never been a better time to be alive on this planet than right now.

www.ingramcontent.com/pod-product-compliance
Lightning Source LLC
Chambersburg PA
CBHW070735020526
44118CB00035B/1363